Stanzaic Guy of Warwick

Middle English Texts

General Editor

Russell A. Peck
University of Rochester

Associate Editor

Alan Lupack
University of Rochester

Assistant Editor

Michael Livingston
University of Rochester

Advisory Board

Rita Copeland
University of Pennsylvania

Thomas G. Hahn
University of Rochester

Lisa Kiser
Ohio State University

R. A. Shoaf
University of Florida

Bonnie Wheeler
Southern Methodist University

The Middle English Texts Series is designed for classroom use. Its goal is to make available to teachers and students texts that occupy an important place in the literary and cultural canon but have not been readily available in student editions. The series does not include those authors, such as Chaucer, Langland, or Malory, whose English works are normally in print in good student editions. The focus is, instead, upon Middle English literature adjacent to those authors that teachers need in compiling the syllabuses they wish to teach. The editions maintain the linguistic integrity of the original work but within the parameters of modern reading conventions. The texts are printed in the modern alphabet and follow the practices of modern capitalization, word formation, and punctuation. Manuscript abbreviations are silently expanded, and *u/v* and *j/i* spellings are regularized according to modern orthography. Yogh is transcribed as *g*, *gh*, *y*, or *s*, according to the letter in modern English spelling to which it corresponds. Distinction between the second person pronoun and the definite article is made by spelling the one *thee* and the other *the*, and final *-e* that receives full syllabic value is accented (e.g., *charité*). Hard words, difficult phrases, and unusual idioms are glossed on the page, either in the right margin or at the foot of the page. Explanatory and textual notes appear at the end of the text, along with a glossary. The editions include short introductions on the history of the work, its merits and points of topical interest, and also contain briefly annotated bibliographies.

Stanzaic Guy of Warwick

Edited by
Alison Wiggins

Published for TEAMS
(The Consortium for the Teaching of the Middle Ages)
in Association with the University of Rochester

by

MEDIEVAL INSTITUTE PUBLICATIONS
College of Arts & Sciences
Western Michigan University
Kalamazoo, Michigan
2004

Library of Congress Cataloging-in-Publication Data

Guy of Warwick (Romance)
  Stanzaic Guy of Warwick / edited by Alison Wiggins.
      p. cm. -- (Middle English texts)
  "Published for TEAMS (The Consortium for the Teaching of the Middle Ages) in
Association with the University of Rochester."
  Includes bibliographical references and index.
  ISBN 1-58044-088-6 (perfectbound : alk. paper)
  1. Guy of Warwick (Legendary character)--Romances. 2. Romances, English. I.
Wiggins, Alison, 1974- II. Title. III. Middle English texts (Kalamazoo, Mich.)
  PR2065.G6 2004
  821'.1--dc22
                                                                   2004018139

ISBN 1-58044-088-6

Copyright 2004 by the Board of Trustees of Western Michigan University

Printed in the United States of America

Cover design by Linda K. Judy

Contents

Acknowledgments

I am very fortunate to have had the late Professor David Burnley as my Ph.D. supervisor, and I continue to be inspired and influenced by the questions he asked about language and history. Sincere thanks go to my colleagues both at the Arts and Humanities Research Board Centre for Editing Lives and Letters and in the School of English, Queen Mary, University of London, who have all offered support, advice, and encouragement during the preparation of this volume. I am also particularly grateful to Professor Peter Brown of the University of Kent who was generous with his time and comments. Thanks must also go to students on the "Pilgrimage" and "Medieval Romance" modules for their perspectives on reading Middle English.

I am grateful to all those on the staff of the Middle English Texts Series for their assistance and encouragement. Special thanks go to Russell A. Peck, who made arrangements for the volume to be included in the series and gave the manuscript an initial reading and critique; to N. M. Heckel for her careful attention to the formatting of the volume and the entering of corrections; and to Michael Livingston, who gave the manuscript its final reading in preparation for submitting it to the Press. I am grateful to Patricia Hollahan and her staff at Medieval Institute Publications for assessing and registering the manuscript. It goes without saying that I alone am responsible for any errors or shortcomings that remain. Finally, I would like to acknowledge the support of the National Endowment for the Humanities for providing the funding that has made this project possible.

Stanzaic Guy of Warwick

Introduction

Summary of the Story

The narrative of the *Stanzaic Guy of Warwick* begins with Guy's return to Warwick after he has established his status as a pre-eminent knight in a series of battles and adventures across Europe. He marries Felice, the daughter of the earl of Warwick and the original inspiration for the conquests in battle that have dominated his life up until this point. Their marriage celebrations last for two weeks, during which time Felice conceives a son (lines 1–228). The festivities are barely over when Guy is suddenly struck by remorse for his past deeds at arms. He repents that he has so long neglected God and is inspired to go on a pilgrimage of atonement. Despite Felice's protestations, and having her assurance that she will not reveal his departure until he is away, he sets off wearing a gold ring from Felice and disguised as a pilgrim. Felice is distressed and only desists from suicide because she knows that she is pregnant and that Guy might be accused of her murder. The next day she tells her father of Guy's departure and search parties are sent out to find him (lines 229–516).

Meanwhile, Guy reaches Jerusalem and Bethlehem, where he visits the holy places. Guy then encounters Earl Jonas and hears of his plight. Jonas tells the story of how he and his fifteen sons had been warring with the Saracen invaders of Jerusalem and, having pursued them into Saracen lands, were outnumbered and imprisoned by King Triamour. During their imprisonment, Triamour's son, Fabour, fought with and killed Sadok, the son of the rich and powerful Sultan. As punishment, the Sultan's court granted Triamour a year and forty days in which to find a champion to match the Sultan's Egyptian giant, Amorant. When asked by Triamour for advice on this matter, Jonas told him that only Guy of Warwick or his companion Herhaud could defeat such a giant. He then made a bargain with Triamour and agreed to bring him Guy or Herhaud within a year in exchange for his liberty and that of his sons. Ever since, Jonas has wandered throughout Europe and the East searching for Guy and Herhaud (lines 517–864). Guy offers to act as Triamour's champion and, though initially put off by Guy's bedraggled appearance, Jonas accepts and presents him to King Triamour in Alexandria. Triamour tells Guy (who uses the pseudonym "Youn") that he should hate him for being an Englishman and a fellow countryman of Guy (who slew his brother and his uncle). Nevertheless, after some speculation about Guy's shabby dress, he accepts him as champion and promises that if he wins he will not only release Jonas and his sons but will liberate and ensure safe passage for

1

all Christian travelers to the Holy Land (lines 865–1056). Guy arms for a battle which takes place in a field encompassed by a river. During the battle Guy grants Amorant leave to drink but, when he asks for the same privilege, is denied unless he reveals his true name. When he hears Guy's name, Amorant is infuriated since Guy in his younger years had wrought such destruction on the Saracen people. Guy makes a desperate dash for the river to drink, then resumes battle, cutting off both Amorant's hands and then his head, which he presents to Triamour, who holds true to his promised rewards. Guy reveals his identity to Jonas before sending him back to his homeland (lines 1057–1683).

Next Guy visits the shrines of Greece and Constantinople. After another long pilgrimage he reaches Germany where he encounters his old friend Tirri, who is in a wretched state. Unrecognized, Guy encourages him to explain the cause of his poverty and distress, and Tirri describes how the Emperor's steward Berard has falsely accused him of the death of his uncle, Duke Otoun (who in fact was slain by Guy during his youth). Tirri tells how he was imprisoned but then, following an appeal to the Emperor by his friends, was released on agreement that he would find and bring Guy to defend him against Berard's accusation. Having searched far and wide, Tirri is now convinced that Guy must be dead. He is full of despair as the time has now come to fulfill his agreement with the Emperor (lines 1684–1896). Guy offers comfort and Tirri has a dream that leads the two of them to a cave of treasure, from which Guy takes a magnificent sword. They head towards court together, but Tirri becomes so fearful that Guy leaves him at an inn and goes on alone. He enters the court as an anonymous pilgrim, angers Berard with reports of his bad reputation abroad, and challenges his treatment of Tirri, whom he then agrees to defend (lines 1897–2136). Guy and Berard are prepared (Berard with a suit of "double" armor and Guy with the sword from the treasure cave), and they engage in a fierce battle. Tirri hides in a church; when he does emerge to view the battle, he is unable to believe that the warrior on the field is the same pilgrim who volunteered to take his part. Evening falls, and it is agreed that the battle will be resumed next morning. During the night, through Berard's treachery, Guy is cast adrift in his bed on the sea and rescued by a fisherman (lines 2137–2400). The Emperor confronts Berard when he finds the pilgrim gone the next morning. However, the fisherman intervenes with the news of his rescue and the battle is resumed until Guy is victorious. Guy goes to tell Tirri the news of Berard's defeat and, after correcting his fears of betrayal, has him instated as steward in place of the treacherous duke. Before departing, Guy reveals his identity to Tirri (lines 2401–2784).

Guy returns to England where he learns that King Athelstan and the English barons are at Winchester praying to God for help against the Danish invaders. The Danes have demanded tribute if no match can be found for their gigantic African champion, Colbrond. No champion for the English comes forward, but that night Athelstan is visited by an angel who tells him that his champion will be the first pilgrim at the north gate of the city the next day. The king follows the angel's instructions and finds Guy, who eventually agrees to take up the fight despite reservations about his own waning physical strength (lines 2785–2976). Guy is armed and prays for divine deliverance. The terms of the battle are set and Colbrond comes forward armed in black steel and with enough weapons to fill a cart. Guy struggles under Colbrond's blows and loses his sword. He makes a dash for Colbrond's stash of weapons and selects a long-handled axe. Colbrond is so enraged that his aim goes awry. When he reaches to retrieve his sword, Guy takes the opportunity to cut off his arm; when he tries again for the weapon, reaching downwards, Guy beheads him. There is great rejoicing among the English, though Guy will accept no reward and asks only for the return of his pilgrim's cloak. Before leaving Guy reveals his identity to Athelstan and elicits from him a promise that he will keep his secret for a year (lines 2977–3324).

Guy joins the poor men fed by Felice at the gates of Warwick Castle and one day is among thirteen invited to eat alongside her. Still unrecognized, he is singled out by Felice for his poor demeanor and offered daily sustenance. However, when the tables are set he leaves. He goes to a hermitage in a nearby forest, where he hopes to receive instruction. When Guy finds the hermit has died, he decides to remain there himself and receives the sacraments daily from a priest. A week before death he is visited by an angel and told to make his final preparations. He sends his page to Felice with her gold ring, and she reaches him on the point of death. A miraculous, sweet smell surrounds Guy after death, and no physical effort can move his body from the hermitage. Felice dies soon after and is buried alongside Guy. When news reaches Tirri, he moves their bodies to Lorraine and has an abbey built where masses are continually sung for Guy and Felice (lines 3325–3576).

Manuscript, Language, and Literary Relations

The source for the *Stanzaic Guy of Warwick* is the Anglo-Norman *Gui de Warewic*, a romance written in England in the thirteenth century (c. 1220) which recounts the story of Guy's life from his earliest years until his death and includes the adventures of his son Reinbroun. It is a vast, ambitious romance and its grand, epic sweep consumes close to thirteen thousand lines. The process of translation into English by the redactor of the *Stanzaic Guy of Warwick* (c. 1300) involved adaptation at a number of different linguistic levels. The redactor limited himself to approximately one-third of the source material, rendering the three and a half thousand or so lines which deal with the story of Guy's later life, from his marriage until his death (*Gui de Warewic*, lines 7409–8974 and 9393–11656). In addition to selecting a specific section of the source, the redactor chose to convert the verse form and rendered the couplet source into twelve-line tail-rhyme stanzas. A number of significant and sometimes revealing adaptations to the content were also made by the redactor (see the Explanatory Notes).

The only extant copy of the *Stanzaic Guy of Warwick* appears in National Library of Scotland Advocates' Manuscript 19.2.1 (known as the Auchinleck Manuscript), folios 146vb–167rb. This manuscript is thought to have been produced in London in the 1330s and is one of the largest and earliest collections of Middle English verse. It is notable not only for its wide-ranging compilation of romances, but also for the variety of other Middle English verse texts it contains, including chronicle, satire, hagiography, and pious instruction.

The *Stanzaic Guy of Warwick* is preceded in the manuscript by a couplet *Guy of Warwick* (folios 108ra–146vb), a romance that deals with the early years of Guy's life, from his childhood role as cupbearer to the earl of Warwick through the subsequent years in which he proves his prowess as a military champion. The stanzaic *Guy*, dealing as it does with the later years of Guy's life, is thus presented as a sequel to the couplet *Guy*. A third installment of the legend then follows: the romance *Reinbroun* (folios 167rb–175vb), which deals with the story of Guy's son. Between them, these three romances cover all the material from the Anglo-Norman source *Gui de Warewic* and present, albeit in piecemeal form, a complete version of the legend in Middle English.

A number of commentators have considered the question of why and how these three texts, with such marked stylistic differences between them, came to be juxtaposed in this manuscript. Carol Fewster approaches the issue from a literary perspective. She draws attention to the way that the pious themes of the latter part of the legend in many ways undermine the values of the first part and as a result offer an ironic commentary on the traditional values of knighthood. Her thesis proposes that the pairing of the couplet and stanzaic texts in the Auchinleck Manuscript was intentionally contrived in order to draw attention to these literary themes. The shift in style and verse form, she argues, brings out contrasts and comparisons between Guy's early and later life that are inherent in and important to the narrative.[1]

The work of Fewster is undoubtedly important for reading the *Stanzaic Guy of Warwick* within the context of the Auchinleck Manuscript. However, there has been a tendency to overstate this kind of reading and only consider the couplet *Guy* and the stanzaic *Guy* in terms of their association with one another. This tendency has been encouraged by Laura Hibbard Loomis' notorious theory (1942) that the Auchinleck Manuscript was produced in a bookshop where texts were translated as well as copied. Her theory is based largely on analysis of the poem and proposes that all three parts were translated simultaneously by a team of poet-scribes who decided to dismantle the source text into three different sections during translation. More recent work on the Auchinleck Manuscript and its texts has shown that Loomis' production theory is untenable and that the manuscript should not be regarded as a bookshop production but as the result of the careful compilation of pre-existing texts.[2] This recognition that Auchinleck was not a collection of new translations but a compilation of available texts (some of which had been in circulation for several decades) is important to understanding the stanzaic

---

[1] Fewster, pp. 85–89.

[2] Timothy A. Shonk, "A Study of the Auchinleck Manuscript: Bookmen and Bookmaking in the Early Fourteenth Century," *Speculum* 60 (1985), 71–91. See also Ikegami, pp. 17–33.

Guy. It shows that, although linked to these other romances in this manuscript, it was originally composed and intended to be read as an independent romance.

It is important not to lose sight of the fact that the stanzaic *Guy* was composed independently and was likely to have circulated and been read on its own elsewhere, that is, without the couplet *Guy* or *Reinbroun*. Study of the language confirms the autonomy of the stanzaic *Guy*: Maldwyn Mills has pointed out that it derives from a version of *Gui de Warewic* different from that of the couplet *Guy* (and that they could not, therefore, have been translated under the same circumstances).[3] Furthermore, whereas the couplet *Guy* was most likely to have been composed in London, examination of the dialect shows that the stanzaic *Guy* was composed in an East Midland dialect. Southern and Eastern influence are suggested by two features: the reflex of OE *y* is regularly <e>, for example, *kende : (hende)* in lines 301–02 and 370–71, and *dent : (went)* in lines 3148–49; and the reflex of OE *ea* before *l*-combinations is <e> or <o>, for example, *welde : beld : (feld : scheld)* in lines 1191, 1194, 1197, and 1200, *bihold : (gold)* in lines 1993–94, and *teld : (feld)* in lines 2107–08. Southern influence is also indicated by instances in rhyme of the verbal suffix *-th* for singular and plural forms of the third person present indicative (lines 724 and 3195). There are also certain relatively unusual lexical forms which seem to have been restricted to East Midland texts, such as *he* ("they," lines 942, 1075, and 3274) and *therkenes* ("darkness," line 1217). Amid this dominant Southern and Eastern coloring, one further feature convincingly indicates an East Midland provenance: certain Northern-derived rhyme sequences are included in which the reflex of OE *ā* is <a>, such as those of the type *sare : ware : (fare : bare)* in lines 573, 576, and 567, 570, respectively. These Northern-derived rhyme sequences are traditional and, in the context of a large number of Southern and Eastern rhymes, should not be regarded as indicative of a Northern provenance but as broadly characteristic of East Midland romance composition. The stylized nature of the language makes it difficult to attempt more precise localization of the dialect. However, as there is nothing in the vocabulary or proportions of forms to suggest the extreme East or North, somewhere in the South Central part of the region, such as Cambridgeshire, is most likely.[4]

The twelve-line tail-rhyme stanza is typical of East Midland romances from this early date, and it determines certain features of their style and tone. Like other stanzaic romances, the

---

[3] Mills, 1991, p. 215.

[4] This analysis takes into consideration the original language of the stanzaic *Guy* and the detailed discussions that are available elsewhere of the dialect of Auchinleck Scribe 1, who copied the text into the manuscript. A profile of Auchinleck Scribe 1's written repertoire, which localizes his dialect within Middlesex, is provided in *A Linguistic Atlas of Late Medieval English*, ed. Angus McIntosh, M. L. Samuels, and Michael Benskin (Aberdeen: Aberdeen University Press, 1986), linguistic profile ("LP") 6510. A slightly different interpretation of the linguistic evidence, which localizes the language of this scribe within London, is offered by M. L. Samuels in his seminal study "Some Applications of Middle English Dialectology," *English Studies* 44 (1963), 81–94; see especially pp. 87–88.

stanzaic *Guy* displays a tendency toward highly patterned phrasing, including alliteration. This is especially so in phrases involving poetic vocabulary (such as "bern," lines 10, 198, 239, 587 and "wede," lines 117, 207, 293, 366, 440, 630, 1065) and in the tail-rhyme position. The tail line regularly contains highly stylized descriptive additions which may be repeated elsewhere in the text or borrowed between romances. The opening stanza, for example, has three tail lines each with conventionalized, alliterating epithets in praise of Guy: "freest founde in fight . . . man most of might . . . Of Warwike wise and wight" (lines 6–12). Similarly, the designation of descriptive formulae to the tail-line position determines the structure of the earl of Warwick's speech to Felice. It here also results in a repeated line, when the same formula is used twice:

> Than seyd th'erl with wordes fre
> "Douhter, yblisced mot thou be
> <u>Of Godes mouthe to mede</u>.
> Ich hadde wele lever than al mi fe
> With than he wald spousy thee,
> <u>That douhti man of dede</u>.
> He hath ben desired of mani woman
> And he hath forsaken hem everilcan,
> <u>That worthly were in wede</u>.
> Ac natheles ichil to him fare
> For to witen of his answare,
> <u>That douhti man of dede</u>." (lines 109–20)

As these examples begin to show, the stanza form encouraged the use of certain techniques, structural patterns, and traditional rhymes and phrases. These can be observed in other stanzaic romances and, broadly speaking, have resulted in a stylistically distinctive corpus. An occasionally lyrical tone is also distinctive among the stanzaic romances, and in the stanzaic *Guy* this can be found in descriptions of nature where simile or metonym are employed:

> Than seighe he an ermine com of his mouthe,
> Als swift as winde that bloweth on clouthe
> As white as lilii on lake (lines 1936–38)

> The sterres on the heven he seighe,
> The water about him drawe.
> Thei he was ferd no wonder it nis;
> Non other thing he no seyghe, ywis,
> Bot winde and wateres wawe. (lines 2348–52)

Introduction

This lyrical tone can be contrasted with the strongly epic-influenced style of the couplet romances produced in London in the early fourteenth century, such as *Kyng Alisaunder*, *Of Arthour and Merlin*, and the couplet *Guy of Warwick*.[5]

Mills has suggested that composition of the stanzaic *Guy* was directly inspired by knowledge of the style and thematic context of another East Midland stanzaic romance, *Amis and Amiloun*:

> The romance of [*Amis and Amiloun*], broadly cognate in tone and in some of its material, first suggested that the final stages of Guy's story should be told as a self-contained romance, and told in tail-rhyme stanzas instead of couplets.[6]

The number of parallels between the stanzaic *Guy* and *Amis and Amiloun* lend plausibility to Mills' proposal.[7] But these similarities of tone should also be seen within the context of a broader interest in themes of piety and long-suffering exhibited among a number of early stanzaic romances. In addition to the stanzaic *Guy* and *Amis and Amiloun*, these include a cluster of stories of the Eustace or Constance type, such as *Octavian*, *Sir Isumbras*, and *The King of Tars*.[8] It was an interest in such themes that gave impetus to the decision of the redactor of the *Stanzaic Guy of Warwick* to focus upon the legend's hagiographic content. Although the identity of the redactor and the earliest readership of the stanzaic *Guy* remain unknown, then, a literary and linguistic community can to some extent be implied. An early fourteenth-century tradition of romance composition, which used the stanza form and was focused upon the East Midlands, was influential in terms of both linguistic procedures and the selection of material. It was as a result of contact with this tradition that the redactor of the stanzaic *Guy* achieved the distinctive tone and the intensified piety which characterizes this version of the romance.[9]

---

[5] Smithers, 1957, pp. 40–55; Wiggins, pp. 222–25.

[6] Mills, 1991, p. 227.

[7] These are listed and discussed in detail by Mills, 1991, Loomis, and W. Möller, *Untersuch-ungen Über Dialekt u. Stil des Mitteleng. Guy of Warwick in der Fassung der Auchinleck-Handschrift u. Über das Verhältnis des Strophischen Teiles des Guy zu der Mitteleng. Romanze Amis und Amiloun*, Ph.D. Dissertation, Konigsberg, 1917, pp. 47–105.

[8] For discussion of the date, provenance, and content of these romances see Severs, vol. 1.

[9] Andrea Hopkins, p. 79, observes in the stanzaic *Guy* "a marked intensification of the pious elements of the Anglo-Norman poem" resulting from the Middle English redactor's alterations to structure and tone. Her chapter on *Guy of Warwick* provides further discussion of this issue. For an example of a specific modification which increases the pious themes of the Middle English redaction, see the note to lines 2353–70 in this edition.

7

Pilgrimage

Every romance involves a journey or quest of some kind. This may be an exile, banishment, separation, seeking of fortune, abduction, abandonment, or a crusade. In the case of the *Stanzaic Guy of Warwick*, the journey is a pilgrimage. The traditional narrative pattern of "exile-and-return," common in romance and folktale, underpins Guy's pilgrimage and is defined around five episodes: (1) the departure from Warwick and journey to the Holy Land, (2) the battle with Amorant in the East, (3) the battle with Berard in Germany, (4) the battle with Colbrond at Winchester, and (5) the return to Warwick and removal to the hermitage. Structural symmetry is maintained by the geographical departure and return to Warwick and the use of parallel characters and episodes (the first and fifth stages both feature Felice; the second and fourth stages both involve a battle with a monstrous opponent).

The adaptation of the well-rehearsed exile-and-return pattern to incorporate a pilgrimage of atonement is the result of the narrative's close association with the *Life of Saint Alexis*. Guy, like Alexis, leaves his wife when newly married in order to pursue a life of pious devotion and poverty in the Holy Land. The *Stanzaic Guy of Warwick* is thus the first Middle English romance in which hagiographical material and themes are incorporated, and (including the other versions of *Guy of Warwick*) it is the one in which their incorporation is most complete.[10] Guy much more closely follows the pattern of a saint's life than the heroes of other so-called penitential romances, like *Sir Isumbras, Sir Gowther*, and *Robert of Cisyle*.[11] He is the only protagonist, for example, who does not re-enter secular society but dies a pilgrim-hermit with posthumous miracles to confirm his spiritual status. And whereas Sir Isumbras, Sir Gowther, and Robert of Cisyle each undertake a pilgrimage as a one-time penitential act, Guy's pilgrimage never ends.

It is the treatment of the pilgrimage motif that to a large extent determines Guy's portrayal and that is used to characterize and idealize his distinctively chivalrous brand of piety. Pilgrimage is by no means an unusual theme in medieval literature, but it receives a particular kind of treatment in the stanzaic *Guy*. In general terms, the presentation of Guy's pilgrimage is underpinned by the well-known theme of the "pilgrimage of life." According to this metaphor, all people are pilgrims exiled from their home who must make their way towards their spiritual goal or homeland and endure hardships and temptation along the way. The three battles Guy undertakes are thus figured as representations of the obstacles or temptations that the Christian pilgrim must overcome on the path of life. This is achieved through the

---

[10] For further discussion of the relationship between *Guy of Warwick* and the *Life of Saint Alexis*, see Dannenbaum, 1984, pp. 357–63, and Klausner, pp. 103–17.

[11] The term "penitential romance" is applied by Hopkins, whose study provides a thorough comparison of this group of Middle English romances.

alternating use of angelic and demonic imagery. In the first battle Guy's opponent is described as a kind of devil: Amorant seems to be "a fende . . . comen . . . out of helle" (lines 743–44), he is "the devels rote" (line 922) or "a devel fram helle" (line 1139), and his sword was "bathed in the flom of Helle" (line 1177). In counterpoint, the second battle figures Guy as an angel: he fights with a sword which shines and flashes like lightning (lines 1988–91) and which he believes was sent to him "fram Heven" (line 1992); those watching the battle say to one another that the "pilgrim was non erthely man; / It was an angel from Heven cam" (lines 2248–49) and conclude that to punish Berard's wickedness God has sent this "angel out of heven-blis" (line 2255). Both strands of imagery come together in the final battle when Guy, bearing a jewel that emanates light and an image of the Three Kings, encounters Colbrond the "fendes fere" (line 3066) whose black armor seems to be that of a "fende of Helle" (line 3060).[12]

The metaphorical and figural potentials of Guy's pilgrimage are made apparent in the text in this way, but there is also a marked interest in the actual pilgrimage that Guy undertakes. Guy first of all visits the shrines and holy places of Jerusalem and Bethlehem. The journey to the Holy Land was the most ambitious, arduous, and exalted of all medieval place pilgrimages.[13] It is therefore remarkable that, having visited the Holy Land, Guy still desires to see more holy places:

> Yete he bithought him sethen tho
> Forto sechen halwen mo
> To winne him heven-mede. (lines 526–28)

He extends his pilgrimage farther around the eastern Mediterranean, to the shrines of Greece and Constantinople. Whilst his pilgrimage exceeds the highest of expectations in terms of its geographical scope, it also exemplifies a method of spiritual scourging through physical hardship. Guy will pay for his sins through bodily suffering:

---

[12] Comparison can be made with the fully developed allegory of pilgrimage presented in *Le Pèlerinage de la Vie Humaine* by Guillaumne de Deguileville (first recension, c. 1330–31), where the pilgrim encounters personified sins and wears a suit of armor symbolizing his Christian virtue. For a discussion of this text and its translation into Middle English prose see *The Pilgrimage of the Lyfe of the Manhode*, ed. Avril Henry, 2 vols., EETS o.s. 288, 292 (Oxford: Oxford University Press, 1985, 1988).

[13] "Place pilgrimage," a term used by Dee Dyas, refers to pilgrimages to holy places, a practice "by no means universally approved and . . . by some regarded as actually harmful to the spiritual life" (pp. 4–5). Dyas differentiates three basic strands of life as pilgrimages: interior pilgrimage (the Contemplative Life — monasticism, anchoritism, meditation, and mysticism), moral pilgrimage (the Active Life, manifesting daily obedience to God and commitment to avoiding the Seven Deadly Sins), and place pilgrimage, to specific sites for general indulgences, healing, or to learn express devotion (p. 6).

That ich have with mi bodi wrought,
With mi bodi it schal be bought
To bote me of that bale. (lines 346–48)

He will walk "barfot" (lines 263, 345) and beg for food (line 264), and the references, as the story progresses, to his gradual dishevelment and deterioration make his physical denial a key feature of the journey.

In these ways an idealized place pilgrimage is depicted. But this is given a further dimension as, simultaneously, Guy's place pilgrimage comes to represent his moral pilgrimage. The idea of a moral pilgrimage involves living out one's prescribed social role, according to one's calling, in the obedient service of God.[14] As a knight, Guy's fulfillment of his social role gains particular emphasis through his success as a crusading figure. His victory in the service of Earl Jonas and King Triamour leads to the release of all Christian prisoners and the granting of free passage for all Christian pilgrims in the Holy Land. This has real significance for a period in which "Saracens" presented a threat to Christian visitors to Jerusalem and when battles over the control of Jerusalem resulted in the crusades.[15] Crusade was itself regarded as a kind of pilgrimage and, again, it is a type of pilgrimage at which Guy excels.

Guy's third and final journey is presented as the culmination of his pilgrimage experience: the interior pilgrimage. Contemporary writing depicts interior pilgrimage as a psychological and emotional journey towards union with God. In contrast to the other kinds of pilgrimage, it is accompanied by physical immobility and social withdrawal. It is this kind of stationary pilgrimage that Guy undertakes in the hermitage and in relative solitude in the final stage of his life. Guy's preparedness for this final pilgrimage is built into the structure of the narrative: there is a gradual decreasing of movement at each stage, and each of Guy's journeys is shorter than the last. Great expanses of land are covered in the first two stages (Warwick to Jerusalem, Constantinople, and Germany), but then each journey contracts as Guy travels from Germany to Winchester, then to Warwick, and finally to the hermitage in a forest outside the city. This correlation between spiritual growth and increased stability is also figured in terms of the shift in Guy's role from one who causes to one who cures wandering. Both Jonas and Tirri wander distressed and lost because they are seeking Guy, and it is Guy who is able to return each to his home and to a position of social stability.

---

[14] The term "moral pilgrimage" is used by Dyas to define this kind of daily obedience; for further discussion of the term, including analysis of its appearance as an important concept is medieval writings, see pp. 6–7 and her chapters on *Piers Plowman* and *The Canterbury Tales*. See note 12, above.

[15] For further discussion of contemporary journeys to Jerusalem and their significance see: Dyas, pp. 236–37, and Colin Morris, "Pilgrimage to Jerusalem in the Late Middle Ages" in Morris and Roberts, pp. 141–63.

Introduction

The stanzaic *Guy* is unusual in its attempt to present and reconcile several different types of pilgrimage within a single narrative. Guy's place pilgrimage is overlaid with his moral pilgrimage and both are followed by an interior pilgrimage. As Dyas observes, these three distinct types of pilgrimage are most often found in tension or conflict with one another in medieval literature and writings.[16] Underlying these tensions was the long-standing debate over place pilgrimage. Critics emphasized the liability of place pilgrimage to abuse, questioned its theological justification, and challenged its relevance alongside versions of pilgrimage which promoted good works and inner virtue. This sense of the inferiority of place pilgrimage can, to some extent, be detected in the *Stanzaic Guy of Warwick*. There is an embedded hierarchy of pilgrimage within the narrative, according to which interior pilgrimage is the superior or higher form. It is no coincidence that it is Guy's final, inner journey which leads him to tread the "redi way . . . to the blis of Heven" (lines 3415 and 3419). However, any real sense of conflict or tension between the different types of pilgrimage is avoided by presenting the interior pilgrimage as the culmination of Guy's journeying. This final journey does not supplant the others, it is prepared for by them.

These idealized notions of pilgrimage are set against the more materialistic attitude to piety voiced by Felice who, attempting to dissuade Guy from departure, tells him that: "Chirches and abbays thou might make / That schal pray for thi sake" (lines 331–32). Whereas Guy is moved by penitential remorse and a desire to make right his individual relationship with God, Felice's piety is based on a more straightforward transaction whereby her charitable donation equates with spiritual merit. The pious behavior of both Guy and Felice conforms to contemporary definitions of orthodoxy, but it is Guy's emphasis upon a personal relationship with God that is promoted and preferred by the narrative.

The presentation of Guy as an ideal or model pilgrim is signaled directly during his final battle when he carries:

A targe listed with gold
Portreyd with thre kinges corn
That present God when he was born,
Mirier was non on mold. (lines 2997–3000)

The Three Kings, who journeyed from the East to pay homage to Christ, are archetypal pilgrims. The image replaces the heraldic arms usually displayed on a shield to identify a knight, and, as such, it makes a bold statement about Guy's identity. Up until this point, Guy has taken the role of pilgrim as a disguise; here, the pilgrim identity has become his own. The development of Guy's identity is central to much of the dramatic irony in the text. It is also

---

[16] See note 12, above.

11

suggestive of Guy's figural potential.[17] He is repeatedly presented as a figure who provokes speculation and inquisition from others, and a number of attempts are made to interpret or decipher his identity from his physical appearance.[18] The public revelation after Guy's death of his dual role as knight and pilgrim-hermit is the occasion for further speculation and confusion. Should he be commemorated with the pomp due to a chivalric knight and military hero, or should his burial reflect his life as an impoverished, pious recluse? Far from being resolved at the end of the narrative, the chaos ensuing over his burial is presented as the closing tableaux. The narrative invites interpretation of the significance of Guy as a pious figure, and the emblem of the Three Kings, model pilgrims, on his shield sets the standard by which he is to be judged.[19]

The significance of Guy as a pious figure has continued to be debated by critics and commentators who have also found that the figures of "ideal knight" and "ideal pilgrim" do not necessarily reside comfortably together.[20] Comments from contemporary churchmen have been used to enforce the assertion that in a number of respects Guy's piety was lacking. There remains, however, no doubt about the widespread popular success of Guy as a pious figure in the two centuries following the composition of the *Stanzaic Guy of Warwick*. The figure of Guy the pilgrim-hermit gives an extra dimension to the *Speculum Gy de Warewick* (that survives in eight manuscripts, including the Auchinleck Manuscript), in which Guy's instruction by the hermit becomes the dramatic frame for a homiletic sermon.[21] Objects associated with Guy's life were held at Winchester Cathedral and described by Gerard of Cornwall and John Lydgate.[22] In fifteenth-century Warwick, a chantry chapel was built in Guy's honor and the supposed location of his "cave" and the "well" from which he drank were

---

[17] Roger Dalrymple, 2000, p. 122, also acknowledges this possibility and argues that the allegorical significances of the narrative are strongly suggested by the language.

[18] Jonas (lines 899–900), Triamour (lines 1003–08), Amorant (lines 1478–88), Tirri (lines 2272–92), and Felice (lines 3361–62) each comment on Guy's appearance or identity and always in a way that involves puzzlement, speculation, and curiosity.

[19] Of particular relevance here is the discussion of "the significance of a knight's coat of arms in relation to his honour or dishonour" and "the relationship of peculiar intimacy between knight and sign" in J. A. Burrow, *Essays on Medieval Literature* (Oxford: Clarendon Press, 1984), chapter 7, "Honour and Shame in *Sir Gawain and the Green Knight*," pp. 122–23.

[20] Dannenbaum, 1984, and Hopkins each offer a detailed consideration of this issue; see also the note to lines 2728–33 in this edition.

[21] *Speculum Gy de Warewyke*, ed. Georgiana Lea Morrill, EETS e.s. 75 (London: Kegan Paul, Trench, Trübner & Co., 1898; rpt. Millwood, NY: Kraus Reprint, 1973).

[22] The objects at Winchester are described in full in the note to line 2794 of this edition.

subsequently discovered.[23] These artifacts, from a range of different geographical regions and social levels, imply how widely known the story of Guy of Warwick the knight turned hermit must have been. They became objects of veneration themselves, objects of pilgrimage, and as such they indicate how the text can itself be seen in part as a promotional document. Above all, they indicate the way in which, by combining the popular motif of pilgrimage with the idealism of romance, the *Stanzaic Guy of Warwick* contributed to the construction of a late medieval cultural icon.

Select Bibliography

Indexed in

IMEV 946.

The Manuscript of the *Stanzaic Guy of Warwick*

Edinburgh, National Library of Scotland, Advocates' MS 19.2.1 (the Auchinleck Manuscript), fols. 146vb–167rb.

Pearsall, Derek, and Ian C. Cunningham, eds. *The Auchinleck Manuscript: National Library of Scotland, Advocates' MS 19.2.1*. London: Scolar Press, 1977. [Facsimile edition.]

Manuscripts Containing Other Redactions of *Guy of Warwick*

Cambridge, Gonville and Caius College MS 107/176.
[c. 1475; couplets. See Zupitza below.]

Cambridge, Cambridge University Library MS Ff.2.38.
[c. 1500; couplets. Edited as a single text, Julius Zupitza, *The Romance of Guy of Warwick: The Second or Fifteenth-Century Version*, EETS e.s. 25–26 (London: Trübner, 1875–76).]

---

[23] Descriptive accounts of the wide-ranging appearances of the figure of Guy of Warwick are provided by Richmond and Ronald Crane.

London, British Library, Sloane MS 1044 (single-folio fragment).
[Fourteenth century; couplets. Edited by Julius Zupitza, "Zur Literaturgeschichte des *Guy of Warwick*," *Sitzungesberichte der Kaiserlichen Akademie der Wissenschaften der Philosophisch-Historische Classe*, 74, no. 1, pp. 623–68.]

Aberystwyth, National Library of Wales MS Binding Fragments 572 and London, British Library MS 14408.
[Early fourteenth century; couplets (fragmentary). See below, Mills and Huws.]

Editions

Burnley, David, and Alison Wiggins, eds. *The Auchinleck Manuscript*. July 2003. National Library of Scotland. <http://www.nls.uk/auchinleck/>

Mills, Maldwyn, and Daniel Huws, eds. *Fragments of an Early Fourteenth-Century Guy of Warwick*. Medium Ævum Monographs n.s. 4. Oxford: Blackwell, 1974.

The Romance of Guy of Warwick: Edited from the Auchinleck Manuscript in the Advocates' Library, Edinburgh, and from MS 107 in Caius College, Cambridge. Ed. Julius Zupitza. 3 vols. EETS e.s. 42, 49, 59. Bungay, UK: Clay and Sons, 1883, 1887, 1891; rpt. London: Oxford University Press, 1966.

Primary Texts

Amis and Amiloun. In *Amis and Amiloun, Robert of Cisyle, and Sir Amadace*. Ed. Edward E. Foster. Kalamazoo, MI: Medieval Institute Publications, 1997.

An Anonymous Short English Metrical Chronicle. Ed. Ewald Zettl. EETS o.s. 196. London: Oxford University Press, 1935. See also Burnley and Wiggins.

Athelston. See *Four Romances of England*.

Bevis of Hampton. See *Four Romances of England*.

Chaucer, Geoffrey. *The Riverside Chaucer*. Third ed. Ed. Larry D. Benson. Boston: Houghton Mifflin, 1987.

Introduction

Floris and Blancheflour. In *Middle English Verse Romances.* Ed. Donald B. Sands. Exeter: Exeter University Press, 1966.

Four Middle English Romances: Sir Isumbras, Octavian, Sir Eglamour of Artois, Sir Tryamour. Ed. Harriet Hudson. Kalamazoo, MI: Medieval Institute Publications, 1996.

Four Romances of England: King Horn, Havelok the Dane, Bevis of Hampton, Athelston. Ed. Ronald B. Herzman, Graham Drake, and Eve Salibury. Kalamazoo, MI: Medieval Institute Publications, 1999.

Gui de Warewic: roman du XIII siècle. Ed. Alfred Ewert. 2 vols. Les Classiques Français du Moyen Age 74–75. Paris: E. Champion, 1933.

Horn Child and Maiden Rimnald. Ed. Maldwyn Mills. Middle English Texts 20. Heidelberg: C. Winter, 1988. See also Burnley and Wiggins.

King Horn. See *Four Romances of England.*

The King of Tars: Edited from the Auchinleck MS, Advocates' 19.2.1. Ed. Judith Perryman. Middle English Texts 12. Heidelberg: C. Winter, 1980. See also Burnley and Wiggins.

Kyng Alisaunder. 2 vols. Ed. G. V. Smithers. 2 vols. EETS o.s. 227, 237. London: Oxford University Press, 1952, 1957; rpt. 1961, 1969.

The Middle English Breton Lays. Ed. Anne Laskaya and Eve Salisbury. Kalamazoo, MI: Medieval Institute Publications, 1995.

Der mittelenglische Vers roman über Richard Löwenherz: Kritische Ausgabe nach allen Handschriften mit Einleitung Anmerkungen und deutscher Ubersetzung [Richard Coer de Lyon]. Ed. Karl Brunner. Wiener Beiträge zur Englischen Philologie 42. Vienna: W. Braumüller, 1913. See also Burnley and Wiggins.

Of Arthour and Merlin. Ed. O. D. Macrae-Gibson. 2 vols. EETS o.s. 268 and 279. London: Oxford University Press, 1973. See also Burnley and Wiggins.

Octavian. See *Four Middle English Romances.*

Reinbroun. See *The Romance of Guy of Warwick.*

Richard Coer de Lyon. See *Der mittelenglische Vers roman über Richard Löwenherz.*

Robert Mannyng of Brunne, The Chronicle. Ed. Idelle Sullens. Medieval and Renaissance Texts and Studies 153. Binghamton, NY: Binghamton University, 1996.

The Seege or Batayle of Troye: A Middle English Metrical Romance. Ed. Mary Elizabeth Barnicle. EETS o.s. 172. London: Oxford University Press, 1927; rpt. New York: Kraus Reprint, 1971.

Short Metrical Chronicle. See *An Anonymous Short English Metrical Chronicle.*

Sir Amadace. See *Amis and Amiloun.*

Sir Cleges. See *The Middle English Breton Lays.*

Sir Eglamour of Artois. See *Four Middle English Romances.*

Sir Gowther. See *The Middle English Breton Lays.*

Sir Isumbras. Ed. James O. Halliwell. In *The Thornton Romances.* Works of the Camden Society 30. London: J. B. Nichols and Son, 1844.

Sir Launfal. See *The Middle English Breton Lays.*

Sir Orfeo. See *The Middle English Breton Lays.*

The Song of Roland. Trans. and intro. Robert L. Harrison. New York: New American Library, 1970.

La Vie de Saint Alexis. Ed. Maurizio Perugi. Textes Littéraires Français 529. Geneva: Droz, 2000.

La Vie de Saint Alexis. Ed. Christopher Storey. Oxford: Blackwell, 1968.

William of Palerne: An Alliterative Romance. Ed. Gerrit H. V. Bunt. Medievalia Groningana 6. Groningen: Bouma's Boekhuis, 1985.

Introduction

Studies

Childress, Diana T. "Between Romance and Legend: 'Secular Hagiography' in Middle English Literature." *Philological Quarterly* 57 (1978), 311–22.

Crane, Ronald S. "The Vogue of *Guy of Warwick* from the Close of the Middle Ages to the Romantic Revival." *PMLA* 30 (1915), 125–94.

Crane, Susan. *Insular Romance: Politics, Faith, and Culture in Anglo-Norman and Middle English Literature.* Berkeley: University of California Press, 1986.

———. "Knights in Disguise: Identity and Incognito in Fourteenth-Century Chivalry." In *The Stranger in Medieval Society.* Ed. F. R. P. Akehurst and Stephanie Cain Van D'Elden. Medieval Cultures 12. Minneapolis: University of Minnesota Press, 1997. Pp. 63–79.

Dalrymple, Roger. "A Liturgical Allusion in *Guy of Warwick.*" *Notes and Queries* n.s. 45 (1998), 27–28.

———. *Language and Piety in Middle English Romance.* Cambridge, UK: D. S. Brewer, 2000.

Dannenbaum, Susan Crane. "*Guy of Warwick* and the Question of Exemplary Romance." *Genre* 17 (1984), 351–74.

Dyas, Dee. *Pilgrimage in Medieval English Literature, 700 – 1500.* Woodbridge, UK: D. S. Brewer, 2001.

Ferris, Sumner. "Chronicle, Chivalric Biography, and Family Tradition in Fourteenth-Century England." In *Chivalric Literature: Essays on Relations between Literature and Life in the Later Middle Ages.* Ed. Larry Dean Benson and John Leyerle. Kalamazoo, MI: Medieval Institute Publications, 1980. Pp. 25–38.

Fewster, Carol. *Traditionality and Genre in Middle English Romance.* Cambridge, UK: D. S. Brewer, 1987.

Field, Rosalind. "Romance as History, History as Romance." In Mills, Fellows, and Meale. Pp. 163–73.

Hopkins, Andrea. *The Sinful Knights: A Study of Middle English Penitential Romance.* Oxford: Clarendon Press, 1990.

Ikegami, Masa T. "The Tripartite Authorship of the Auchinleck *Guy of Warwick.*" *Kyoyo-Ronso* 78 (1988), 17–33.

Klausner, David N. "Didacticism and Drama in *Guy of Warwick.*" *Medievalia et Humanistica* n.s. 6 (1975), 103–19.

Krueger, Roberta L. *The Cambridge Companion to Medieval Romance.* Cambridge, UK: Cambridge University Press, 2000.

Legge, M. Dominica. *Anglo-Norman Literature and Its Background.* Oxford: Clarendon Press, 1963.

———. "Anglo-Norman Hagiography and the Romances." *Medievalia et Humanistica* n.s. 6 (1975), 41–49.

Loomis, Laura Hibbard. "The Auchinleck Manuscript and a Possible London Bookshop of 1330–1340." *PMLA* 57 (1942), 595–627. Rpt. in *Adventures in the Middle Ages: A Memorial Collection of Essays and Studies.* New York: B. Franklin, 1962. Pp. 150–87.

Mason, Emma. "Legends of the Beauchamps' Ancestors: The Use of Baronial Propaganda in Medieval England." *Journal of Medieval History* 10 (1984), 25–40.

Mills, Maldwyn. "Techniques of Translation in the Middle English Versions of *Guy of Warwick.*" In *The Medieval Translator II.* Ed. Roger Ellis. Westfield Publications in Medieval Studies 5. London: Centre for Medieval Studies, Queen Mary and Westfield College, University of London, 1991. Pp. 209–29.

———. "Structure and Meaning in *Guy of Warwick.*" In *From Medieval to Medievalism.* Ed. John Simons. New York: St. Martin's Press, 1992. Pp. 54–68.

Mills, Maldwyn, Jennifer Fellows, and Carol M. Meale, eds. *Romance in Medieval England.* Cambridge, UK: Brewer, 1991.

Morris, Colin, and Peter Roberts, eds. *Pilgrimage: The English Experience from Becket to Bunyan.* Cambridge, UK: Cambridge University Press, 2002.

Richmond, Velma Bourgeois. *The Legend of Guy of Warwick.* Garland Studies in Medieval Literature 14. New York: Garland, 1996.

Smithers, G. V. "The Style of *Hauelok.*" *Medium Ævum* 57 (1988), 190–218.

Stopford, Jennie, ed. *Pilgrimage Explored.* Woodbridge, UK: York Medieval Press, 1999.

Weiss, Judith. "Emperors and Antichrists: Reflections of Empire in Insular Narrative, 1130–1250." In *The Matter of Identity in Medieval Romance.* Ed. Phillipa Hardman. Woodbridge, UK: D. S. Brewer, 2002. Pp. 87–102.

Wiggins, Alison. "*Guy of Warwick* in Warwick?: Reconsidering the Dialect Evidence." *English Studies* 84 (2003), 219–30.

Woolgar, C. M. *The Great Household in Late Medieval England.* New Haven, CT: Yale University Press, 1999.

Common Reference Works

Bordman, Gerald Martin. *Motif-Index of the English Metrical Romances.* Helsinki: Suomalainen Tiedeakatemia, 1963.

Borland, Katherine R., ed. *A Descriptive Catalogue of the Western Mediaeval Manuscripts in Edinburgh University Library.* Edinburgh: Edinburgh University Press, 1916.

Brown, Carleton, and Rossell Hope Robbins, eds. *The Index of Middle English Verse.* New York: Columbia University Press, 1943.

Farmer, David Hugh, ed. *The Oxford Dictionary of Saints.* Oxford: Clarendon Press, 1978.

Kurath, Hans, and Sherman M. Kuhn, eds. [Ed. Sherman M. Kuhn and S. Reidy after 1965]. *Middle English Dictionary.* Ann Arbor: University of Michigan Press, 1952–2003.

Severs, J. Burke, gen. ed. *Manual of the Writings in Middle English 1050–1500.* Vols. 1–5. New Haven: Connecticut Academy of Arts and Sciences, 1967.

Storey, Christopher. *An Annotated Bibliography and Guide to Alexis Studies (La Vie de saint Alexis).* Histoire des idées et critique littéraire 251. Geneva: Droz, 1987.

Whiting, Bartlett Jere, with the collaboration of Helen Wescott Whiting. *Proverbs, Sentences, and Proverbial Phrases from English Writings Mainly before 1500*. Cambridge, MA: The Belknap Press of Harvard University Press, 1968.

Stanzaic Guy of Warwick

	God graunt hem heven-blis to mede	
	That herken to mi romaunce rede[1]	
	Al of a gentil knight;	*All about*
	The best bodi he was at nede	*person; in time of danger*
5	That ever might bistriden stede	*ride a horse*
	And freest founde in fight.	*most noble*
	The word of him ful wide it ran	
	Over al this warld the priis he wan,	*reputation*
	As man most of might.	
10	Balder bern was non in bi,	*[A] bolder man; town*
	His name was hoten Sir Gii	*called*
	Of Warwike wise and wight.	*clever; courageous*
	Wight he was for sothe to say	*Valiant; to tell the truth*
	And holden for priis in everi play	*most excellent; tournament*
15	As knight of gret boundé.	*valor*
	Out of this lond he went his way	
	Thurth mani divers cuntray	
	That was biyond the see.	
	Sethen he com into Inglond	*Afterwards*
20	And Athelston the king he fond	
	That was bothe hende and fre.	*noble*
	For his love ich understond	*I*
	He slough a dragoun in Northhumberlond	
	Ful fer in the north cuntré.	
25	He and Herhaud for sothe to say	
	To Wallingforth toke the way	
	That was his faders toun.	
	Than was his fader sothe to say	

---

[1] Lines 1–2: *God give them the rewards of heaven / Who listen to my romance read aloud*

Ded and birid in the clay;
30   His air was Sir Gioun.   *heir*
Alle that held of him lond or fe   *property*
Deden him omage and feuté   *allegiance; fealty*
And com to his somoun.   *command*
He tok alle his faders lond
35   And gaf it hende Herhaud in hond   *noble; into his possession*
Right to his warisoun.   *reward*

And alle that hadde in his servise be
He gaf hem gold and riche fe   *gave; payment*
Ful hendeliche on honde   *nobly*
40   And sethen he went with his meyné   *then; retinue*
To th'erl Rohaud that was so fre,   *noble*
At Warwike he him fond.
Alle than were thai glad and blithe   *joyful; pleased*
And thonked God a thousand sithe   *times*
45   That Gii was comen to lond.
Sethe on hunting thai gun ride   *Then; did*
With knightes fele and miche pride   *many; much*
As ye may understond.

On a day Sir Gii gan fond   *began his attempt*
50   And feir Felice he tok bi hond
And seyd to that bird so blithe   *fair lady*
"Ichave," he seyd, "thurth Godes sond   *I have; through God's grace*
Won the priis in mani lond   *victory*
Of knightes strong and stithe   *valiant*
55   And me is boden gret anour,   *offered; honor*
Kinges douhter and emperour,   *daughters*
To have to mi wive.
Ac swete Felice," he seyd than,   *But*
"Y no schal never spouse wiman   *marry*
60   Whiles thou art olive."

Than answerd that swete wight   *woman*
And seyd ogain to him ful right   *in reply; directly*
"Bi Him that schope mankinne,   *made*
Icham desired day and night   *I am*

65	Of erl, baroun, and mani a knight;	
	For nothing wil thai blinne.	*cease*
	Ac Gii," sche seyd, "hende and fre,	*gentle; noble*
	Al mi love is layd on thee,	
	Our love schal never tuinne;	*end*
70	And bot ich have thee to make	
	Other lord nil Y non take	
	For al this warld to winne."[1]	
	Anon to hir than answerd Gii,	*Soon*
	To fair Felice that sat him bi	*beside*
75	That semly was of sight,	*beautiful was to behold*
	"Leman," he seyd, "gramerci."	*Sweetheart; many thanks*
	With joie and with melodi	*delight*
	He kist that swete wight.	*woman*
	Than was he bothe glad and blithe,	
80	His joie couthe he no man kithe	
	For that bird so bright.[2]	
	He no was never therbiforn	
	Half so blithe sethe he was born	
	For nought that man him hight.[3]	
85	On a day th'erl gan fond	*the earl (i.e., Felice's father)*
	And fair Felice he tok bi hond	
	And hir moder biside,	
	"Douhter," he seyd, "now understond	*Daughter*
	Why wiltow have non husbond	*will you*
90	That might thee spouse with pride?	*splendor*
	Thou has ben desired of mani man	*men*
	And yete no wostow never nan	
	For nought that might bitide.[4]	

---

[1] Lines 70–72: *Unless I have you as my husband / I will not take another man / For all the riches in the world*

[2] Lines 80–81: *His happiness he could explain to no one / On account of that beautiful woman*

[3] Lines 82–84: *He had never before been / Half so joyful since he was born / For anything that anyone had promised him*

[4] Lines 92–93: *And yet you will not take [as a husband] one of them / Under any circumstance*

	Leve douhter hende and fre	*Dear*
95	Telle me now *par charité*	
	What man thou wilt abide."	*accept*

	Felice answerd ogain	
	"Fader," quath hye, "ichil thee sain	*she; tell*
	With wordes fre and hende.	
100	Fader," quath sche, "ichil ful fayn	*I will very willingly*
	Tel thee at wordes tuain	*in two words*
	Bi Him that schop mankende.	*created*
	Opon Sir Gii that gentil knight,	
	Ywis, mi love is alle alight	*In truth*
105	In warld where that he wende	
	And bot he spouse me, at o word,	*wed; in a word (in short)*
	Y no kepe never take lord,	*I will never obey or accept a husband*
	Day withouten ende."	

	Than seyd th'erl with wordes fre,	*frank*
110	"Douhter, yblisced mot thou be	*blessed must*
	Of Godes mouthe to mede.	*as reward*
	Ich hadde wele lever than al mi fe	*much rather*
	With than he wald spousy thee,	*At once*
	That douhti man of dede.	*noble; deed*
115	He hath ben desired of mani woman	
	And he hath forsaken hem everilcan,	*declined them each and every one*
	That worthly were in wede.	*Who honorable; in clothing*
	Ac natheles ichil to him fare	*nonetheless*
	For to witen of his answare,	
120	That douhti man of dede."	

	On a day withouten lesing	*lying*
	Th'erl him rode on dere hunting	*deer*
	And Sir Gii the conquerour,	
	Als thai riden on her talking	*their*
125	Thai speken togider of mani thing,	
	Of levedis bright in bour.	*ladies beautiful in chamber*
	Th'erl seyd to Sir Gii hende and fre,	
	"Tel me the sothe *par charité*	
	Y pray thee, *par amoure,*	*if you please (of your kindness)*

24

130	Hastow ment ever in thi live	*Have you ever intended*
	Spouse ani wiman to wive	
	That falleth to thine anour?"	*comes within your high rank*
	Sir Gii answerd and seyd than	
	"Bi Him," he seyd, "that this warld wan	*won (saved)*
135	To saven al mankende,	
	Bi nought that Y tel can	
	Y nil never spouse wiman	
	Save on is fre and hende."	*Except one [who] is*
	"Sir," quath th'erl, "listen nou to me:	
140	Y have a douhter bright on ble,	*fair of face*
	Y pray thee leve frende,	*dear*
	To wive wiltow hir understond	*take*
	Y schal thee sese in al mi lond	*make you legal possessor of*
	To hold withouten ende."	
145	"Gramerci," seyd Gii anon,	
	"So help me Crist and Seyn Jon	*Saint*
	And Y schuld spouse a wive	
	Ich hadde lever hir bodi alon	
	Than winnen al this warldes won	
150	With ani woman o live."[1]	
	Than seyd th'erl, "Gramerci,"	
	And in his armes he kist Sir Gii	
	And thonked him mani a sithe.	*time*
	"Sir Gii," he seyd, "thou art mi frende,	
155	Now thou wilt spouse mi dohter hende	
	Was Y never are so blithe."	*before*
	"Ac certes," seyd th'erl so fre,	*certainly*
	"Sir Gii, yif thou wilt trowe me	*if; put your confidence in me*
	No lenger thou no schalt abide.	*wait*
160	Now for fourtenight it schal be	*in two weeks*
	The bridal hold with gamen and gle	*entertainments; pleasure*

---

[1] Lines 148–50: *I would rather have her alone / Than gain all worldly goods / With any other woman alive*

25

At Warwike in that tyde."   *time*
Than was Sir Gii glad and blithe
His joie couthe he no man kithe,   *express to no man*
165   To his ostel he gan ride.   *lodgings*
And tho Gii com hom to his frende   *when*
He schuld spouse his douhter hende   *(i.e. the earl's)*
He teld Herhaud that tide.

Th'erl Rouhaud as swithe dede sende   *at once*
170   After lordinges fer and hende   *nobles; near*
That pris wel told in tour,   *honorable event*
When the time was comen to th'ende   *allotted period*
To chirche wel feir gun thai wende   *very courteously*
With mirthe and michel anour.
175   Miche semly folk was gadred thare
Of erls, barouns, lasse and mare,
And levedis bright in bour.   *ladies beautiful; chamber*
Than spoused Sir Gii that day
Fair Felice that miri may   *maid*
180   With joie and gret vigour.   *eagerness*

When he hadde spoused that swete wight
The fest lasted a fourtennight
That frely folk in fere   *Those freeborn; together*
With erl, baroun, and mani a knight
185   And mani a levedy fair and bright
The best in lond that were.   *finest (highest in rank)*
Ther wer giftes for the nones,   *for the occasion*
Gold and silver and precious stones
And druries riche and dere.   *treasures (keepsakes)*
190   Ther was mirthe and melody
And al maner menstracie   *musical performance*
As ye may fortheward here.

Ther was trumpes and tabour,   *horn players; drummers*
Fithel, croude, and harpour   *fiddlers, croude players; harpers*
195   Her craftes for to kithe;   *Their skills; show*
Organisters and gode stivours,   *Organists; bagpipers*
Minstrels of mouthe and mani dysour   *Singers (Story-tellers); entertainers (jesters)*

26

	To glade tho bernes blithe.	*please those people*
	Ther nis no tong may telle in tale	*is not any tongue*
200	The joie that was at that bridale	
	With menske and mirthe to mithe,	*hospitality; pleasure to be seen*
	For ther was al maner of gle	*entertainment*
	That hert might thinke other eyghe se	*imagine or eye see*
	As ye may list and lithe.	*listen and hear*
205	Herls, barouns, hende and fre	*Earls*
	That ther war gadred of mani cuntré	
	That worthliche were in wede,	*honorable; in clothing*
	Thai goven glewemen for her gle	*gave professional entertainers; their*
	Robes riche, gold and fe,	
210	Her giftes were nought gnede.	*stingy*
	On the fiftenday ful yare	*right away*
	Thai toke her leve for to fare	
	And thonked hem her gode dede.	*kindness*
	Than hadde Gii that gentil knight	
215	Feliis to his wil day and night	*at his desire*
	In gest also we rede.	*story as*
	When Gii hadde spoused that hendy flour,	*noble woman*
	Fair Feliis so bright in bour	
	That was him leve and dere,	*[to] him*
220	Ywis, in Warwike in that tour	
	Fiftendays with honour	
	With joie togider thai were.	
	So it bifel that first night	
	That he neyghed that swete wight	*knew sexually*
225	A child thai geten yfere	*together*
	And sethen with sorwe and sikeing sare	*But afterwards; painful sighing*
	Her joie turned hem into care	*Their; them; sadness*
	As ye may forward here.	*henceforth hear*
	Than was Sir Gii of gret renoun	*reputation*
230	And holden lord of mani a toun	*[was] regarded as lord*
	As prince proude in pride.	*magnificent in array (splendidly dressed)*
	That Erl Rohaut and Sir Gyoun	
	In fretthe to fel the dere adoun	*park (woodland) to slay deer*

27

On hunting thai gun ride.

235   It bifel opon a somers day
      That Sir Gii at Warwike lay —
      In herd is nought to hide —   *It is no secret (It is well known)*
      At night in tale as it is told
      To bedde went tho bernes bold   *those*
240   Bi time to rest that tide.   *At that time; then*

      To a turet Sir Gii is went
      And biheld that firmament   *sky (heaven)*
      That thicke with steres stode,   *crowded; stars*
      On Jhesu omnipotent
245   That alle his honour hadde him lent   *glory; granted*
      He thought with dreri mode,   *downcast mood*
      Hou he hadde ever ben strong werrour,   *always; warrior*
      For Jhesu love, our Saveour,
      Never no dede he gode.[1]
250   Mani man he hadde slayn with wrong;   *without just cause*
      "Allas, allas!" it was his song,
      For sorwe he yede ner wode.   *He nearly went mad with remorse*

      "Allas," he seyd, "that Y was born,
      Bodi and soule icham forlorn,   *(i.e., damned to hell)*
255   Of blis icham al bare   *I am stripped of all joy*
      For never in al mi liif biforn
      For Him that bar the croun of thorn
      Gode dede dede Y nare.   *deed did; none*
      Bot wer and wo ichave don wrought   *war; distress I have caused*
260   And mani a man to grounde ybrought,
      That rewes me ful sare.   *grieves; severely*
      To bote min sinnes ichil wende   *cure; I shall*
      Barfot to mi lives ende   *Barefoot*
      To bid mi mete with care."   *beg; food*

265   As Gii stode thus in tour alon
      In hert him was ful wo bigon,   *overcome with grief*

---

[1] Lines 248–49: *[But] for love of Jesus, our Savior, / He had never done any good deeds*

28

	"Allas!" it was his song.	
	Than com Feliis sone anon	
	And herd him make rewely mon	*pitiful cries*
270	With sorwe and care among.	*continually*
	"Leman," sche seyd, "what is thi thought?	*Lover; distress*
	Whi artow thus in sorwe brought?	
	Me thenke thi pain wel strong.	*[is] very severe*
	Hastow ought herd of me bot gode[1]	
275	That thou makes thus dreri mode?	
	Ywis, thou hast gret wrong."	*Truly; injustice*
	"Leman," seyd Gii ogain,	*in answer*
	"Ichil thee telle the sothe ful fain	*I shall; willingly*
	Whi icham brought to grounde.	
280	Sethen Y thee seyghe first with ayn —	*saw you; eyes*
	Allas the while Y may sayn —	*time; say*
	Thi love me hath so ybounde	*ensnared*
	That never sethen no dede Y gode[2]	
	Bot in wer schadde mannes blode	*shed*
285	With mani a griseli wounde.	*grisly*
	Now may me rewe al mi live	
	That ever was Y born o wive	*of woman*
	Wayleway that stounde!"	*Alas; moment*
	"Ac yif ich hadde don half the dede	*But if*
290	For Him that on Rode gan blede	*Cross*
	With grimly woundes sare,	*severe; painful*
	In Hevene He wald have quit mi mede	*given my reward*
	In joie to won with angels wede	*live in angels' clothing*
	Evermore withouten care.	
295	Ac for thi love ich have al wrought,[3]	
	For His love dede Y never nought;	
	Jhesu amende mi fare.	*put right my course*
	Therfore ich wot that icham lorn.	*know; lost*

---

[1] *Have you heard anything at all about me that is not good*

[2] *That I never did any virtuous acts after that moment*

[3] *But everything I have done has been for your love*

29

Allas the time that Y was born,
300 Of blis icham al bare.

"Bot God is curteys and hende
And so dere he hath bought mankende   *dearly; saved*
For no thing wil hem lete.   *abandon*
For His love ichil now wende   *walk*
305 Barfot to mi lives ende
Mine sinnes forto bete   *to atone [for]*
That whoreso Y lye anight   *wherever; at night*
Y schal never be seyn with sight   *recognized*
Bi way no bi strete.   *Along road nor*
310 Of alle the dedes Y may do wel,
God graunt thee, lef, that halvendel[1]
And Marie His moder swete."

Than stode that hende levedi stille   *noble lady*
And in hir hert hir liked ille   *was distressed*
315 And gan to wepe anon.
"Leman," sche seyd, "what is thi wille?
Ywis, thi speche wil me spille.   *kill*
Y not what Y may don.   *know not*
Y wot thou hast in sum cuntré   *believe*
320 Spoused another woman than me
That thou wilt to hir gon   *And*
And now thou wilt fro me fare.
Allas, allas, now cometh mi care!
For sorwe ichil me slon.   *I shall slay myself*

325 "For wer and wo thatow hast wrought   *that you*
God that al mankende hath bought,
So curteys He is and hende,
Schrive thee wele in word and thought   *Absolve you*
And than thee tharf dout right nought   *need not feel fearful*
330 Ogaines the foule fende.   *In the presence of the devil*

---

[1] Lines 310–11: *Of all the good deeds that I may accomplish, / I ask God to grant to you, my dear, half the benefit of them*

Chirches and abbays thou might make
That schal pray for thi sake
To Him that schope mankende.
Hastow no nede to go me fro;
335   Save thou might thi soule fram wo   *misery*
In joie withouten ende."

"Leve leman," than seyd Sir Gii,   *Dear darling*
"Lete ben alle this reweful cri;
It is nought worth thi tale.   *concern*
340   For mani a bern and knight hardi   *brave*
Ich have ysleyn sikerly   *assuredly*
And strued cites fale   *destroyed; many*
And for ich have destrued mankin   *because; many people*
Y schal walk for mi sinne
345   Barfot bi doun and dale.   *hill*
That ich have with mi bodi wrought,   *What*
With mi bodi it schal be bought
To bote me of that bale.   *cure; misery*

"Leman," he seyd, "*par charité*,
350   Astow art bothe hende and fre   *As you*
O thing Y thee pray: *One; entreat*
Loke thou make no sorwe for me   *See to it that*
Bot hold thee stille astow may be   *inconspicuous (silent)*
Til tomorwe at day.
355   Gret wele thi fader that is so hende
And thi moder and al thi frende   *friends*
Bi sond as Y thee say;   *a messenger*
Grete wele Herhaud Y thee biseche;
Leman, God Y thee biteche,   *to God I entrust you*
360   Y wil fare forth in mi way.

"Leman, Y warn thee biforn   *in advance*
With a knave child thou art ycorn   *boy; favored*
That douhti beth of dede.
For Him that bar the croun of thorn,
365   Therfore, as sone as it is born   *he*
Pray Herhaud wight in wede

31

	He teche mi sone as he wele can	
	Al the thewes of gentil man	*customs (qualities)*
	And helpe him at his nede.	*in times of trouble*
370	For he is bothe gode and hende	
	And ever he hath ben trewe and kende,	*faithful; constant*
	God quite him his mede.	*reward*
	"Leman," he seyd, "have here mi brond	*sword*
	And take mi sone it in his hond	*give*
375	Astow art hende and fre,	
	He may therwith ich understond	
	Winne the priis in everi lond	*victory*
	For better may non be.	
	Leman," he seyd, "have now godeday.	
380	Ichil fare forth in mi way	
	And wende in mi jurné."	*go; journey*
	Thai kist hem in armes tuo	
	And bothe thai fel aswon tho —	*then*
	Gret diol it was to se.	*sadness*
385	Gret sorwe thai made at her parting	*their*
	And kist hem with eyghen wepeing,	*eyes*
	Bi the hond sche gan him reche	*grasped him*
	"Leman," sche seyd, "have here this ring;	
	For Jhesus love heven-king	
390	A word Y thee biseche:	
	When thou ert in fer cuntré	*are*
	Loke heron and thenk on me	*here upon*
	And God Y thee biteche."	*God be with you*
	With that word he went hir fro	
395	Wepeand with eyghen to	*Weeping; two*
	Withouten more speche.	
	Now is Gii fram Warwike fare,	*gone*
	Unto the se he went ful yare	*quickly*
	And passed over the flod.	*sea*
400	The levedy bileft at hom in care	*remained*
	With sorwe and wo and sikeing sare;	*sighing*
	Wel drery was hir mode.	

"Allas, allas," it was hir song,
Hir here sche drough, hir hond sche wrong,   *hair; tore; hands; wrung*
405 Hir fingres brast o blode.   *bled profusely*
Al that night til it was day
Hir song it was, "wayleway,"
For sorwe sche yede ner wode.   *went nearly mad*

Hir lordes swerd sche drough biforn   *drew*
410 And thought have slain hirself for sorn   *out of sorrow*
Withouten more delay.
To sle hirselven er the child wer born   *before*
Sche thought hir soule it wer forlorn   *it would be lost*
Evermore at Domesday,   *Forever*
415 And that hir fader hir frendes ichon
Schuld seyn hir lord it hadde ydon
And were so fled oway.[1]
Therfore sche dede his swerd ogain   *put away*
Elles for sorwe sche hadde hir slain   *herself*
420 In gest as Y you say.

Arliche amorwe when it was day   *Early in the morning*
To chaumber ther hir fader lay   *where*
Sche com wringand hir hond.   *wringing; hands*
"Fader," sche seyd, "ichil thee say
425 Mi lord is went fro me his way
In pilgrimage to fond.   *undertake*
He wil passe over the se,
Schal he never com to me   *He shall*
Ogain into Inglond."
430 For sorwe that sche hadde that stounde
Aswon sche fel adoun to grounde,   *at that time*
O fot no might sche stonde.   *On foot*

"Douhter," seyd hir fader, "lat be,   *desist [from sorrow]*
Y trowe nought that Sir Gii the fre   *think not; noble*

---

[1] Lines 415–17: *And [she thought] that her father and each of her friends / Would say that her husband had done it / And had therefore fled away*

33

435	Is thus fram thee fare.	
	Ywis, he nis nought passed the se;	
	He ne doth nought bot forto fond thee	*test*
	Hou trewe of hert thou ware."	
	"Nay, sir," sche seyd, "so God me spede,	*assist*
440	He is walked in pouer wede	*poor*
	To beggen his mete with care	
	And therfore now singen Y may	
	Allas the time and wayleway	
	That mi moder me bare."	

445	Th'erl ros up with sikeing sare	*sighing*
	For Sir Gii was fram him fare,	*Because*
	In hert him was ful wo	
	And alle his frendes, lesse and mare,	
	For Sir Gii thai hadde gret care	*On account of*
450	For he was went hem fro.	
	Thai sought him than al about	
	Within the cité and without	
	Ther he was won to go.	*accustomed*
	And when thai founde him nought that day	
455	Ther was mani a "wayleway"	
	Wringand her hondes tuo.	*Wringing their*

	And when Gii was fram hem gon	
	Herhaud and his frendes ichon	*each one*
	And other barouns him by	
460	To th'erl Rohaut thai seyden anon,	
	"The best rede that we can don	*plan; devise*
	Smertliche and hastily,	*Rapidly*
	Messangers we schul now sende	
	Over alle this lond fer and hende	*near*
465	To seche mi lord Sir Gii	
	And yif he be nought in this lond	*if*
	He is in Loreyn ich understond	*Lorraine; imagine (assume)*
	With his brother Tirry."	*close friend*

	Menssangers anon thai sende
470	Over al this lond fer and hende

Fram Londen into Louthe
Over al biyonde Humber and Trent
And est and west thurthout al Kent
To the haven of Portesmouthe.   *harbor*
475   Thai sought him over al up and doun
Over alle the lond in everich toun   *every*
Bi costes that wer couthe   *regions; familiar*
And sethen to Warwike thai gan wende   *then; return*
And seyd thai might him nowhar fende
480   Bi north no bi southe.

Herhaud was wele understond   *accurately concluded*
That Gii was fer in uncouthe lond.   *foreign*
Ful hende he was and fre,
Palmers wede he tok on hond   *Pilgrim's clothes*
485   To seche his lord he wald fond   *seek*
Unto the Grekis See.   *Mediterranean*
To th'erl Rohaut he seyd anon
To seche his lord he most gon
Thurth alle Cristianté.   *Christendom*
490   When th'erl seye him thus ydight   *saw; dressed*
"Thou art," he seyd, "a trewe knight,
Yblisced mot thou be."   *Blessed*

Tho went Herhaud so trewe in tale   *honest in speech*
To seche his lord in londes fale,   *many*
495   For nothing he nold abide;   *delay*
He yede over alle bi doun and dale
To everi court and kinges sale   *hall*
Bi mani a lond side.   *Across; country border*
Thurth Normondye and alle Speyne   *Through*
500   Into Fraunce and thurth Breteyne   *Brittany*
He yede bothe fer and wide;   *went*
Thurth Lorain and thurth Lombardye
And never no herd he telle of Gii   *never heard anything spoken*
For nought that might bitide.   *Not in any circumstance*

505   When Herhaud had sought him fer and hende
And he no might him nowhar fende,   *find*

35

	Noither bi se no sond,	*sea nor land*
	Into Inglond he gan wende	
	And th'erl Rohaut and al his frende	
510	At Warwike he hem fond,	*met*
	And teld he hadde his lord sought	*told [them how]*
	And that he no might finde him nought	
	In nonskinnes lond.	*no kinds of*
	Mani a moder child that day	
515	Wepe and gan say, "waileway,"	
	Wel sore wringand her hond.	*hands*
	Now herken and ye may here	*listen*
	In gest yif ye wil listen and lere	*[the] story if; learn*
	Hou Gii as pilgrim yede.	*went*
520	He welke about with glad chere	*walked; contented mood*
	Thurth mani londes fer and nere	
	Ther God him wald spede.	*Wherever God would guide him*
	First he went to Jerusalem	
	And sethen he went to Bedlem	*then; Bethlehem*
525	Thurth mani an uncouthe thede.	*foreign country*
	Yete he bithought him sethen tho	*Nonetheless; then decided*
	Forto sechen halwen mo	*To seek out more shrines*
	To winne him heven-mede.	*To win for himself the rewards of heaven*
	Tho he went his pilgrimage	*Then; continued*
530	Toward the court of Antiage,	*Antioch*
	Bi this half that cité	*On this side of*
	He mett a man of fair parage,	*high rank*
	Ycomen he was of heyghe linage	*noble ancestry*
	And of kin fair and fre.	*high-born*
535	Michel he was of bodi ypight,	*Large; with a well-built body*
	A man he semed of michel might	*great strength*
	And of gret bounté	*prowess*
	With white hore heved and berd yblowe[1]	
	As white as ani driven snowe;	
540	Gret sorwe than made he.	

---

[1] *With a greyish-white head [of hair] and plentiful beard*

So gret sorwe ther he made
Sir Gii of him rewthe hade   *pity*
He gan to wepe so sare.
His cloth he rent, his here totorn,   *clothes; ripped; hair tore to shreds*
545 And curssed the time that he was born
Wel diolful was his fare;   *behavior*
More sorwe made never man.
Gii stode and loked on him than
And hadde of him gret care.   *concern*
550 He seyd, "Allas and walewo,
Al mi joie it is ago,   *gone*
Of blis icham al bare."

"Gode man, what artow," seyd Gii,   *what [type of person] are you*
"That makest thus this reweful cri   *piteous*
555 And thus sorweful mone?
Me thenke for thee icham sori   *for your sake*
For that thine hert is thus drery,   *sorrowful*
Thi joie is fro thee gon.
Telle me the sothe Y pray thee
560 For Godes love in Trinité
That this world hath in won.   *has lived in*
For Jhesu is of so michel might   *power*
He may make thine hert light   *joyful*
And thou not never hou son."   *know not; soon*

565 "Gode man," seyd the pilgrim,
"Thou hast me frained bi God thin   *asked; your God*
To telle thee of mi fare   *behavior*
And alle the soth withouten les   *truth; lies*
Ichil thee telle hou it wes   *was*
570 Of blis hou icham bare.
So michel sorwe is on me steke   *afflicted*
That min hert it wil tobreke
With sorwe and sikeing sare.
Forlorn ich have al mi blis
575 Y no schal never have joie, ywis,
In erthe Y wald Y ware.   *I wish I were in the earth [i.e., my grave]*

"A man Y was of state sum stounde   *rank at one time*
And holden a lord of gret mounde   *regarded; importance*
And erl of al Durras.
580   Fair sones ich hadde fiftene
And alle were knightes stout and kene;   *strong; brave*
Men cleped me th'erl Jonas.   *called*
Y trowe in this warld is man non,   *believe*
Ywis, that is so wo bigon
585   Sethen the world made was,   *Since*
For alle min sones ich have forlorn —   *lost*
Better berns were non born —   *men*
Therfore Y sing 'allas.'

"For blithe worth Y never more: *happy I will never be again*
590   Alle mi sones ich have forlore
Thurth a batayl unride,   *violent*
Thurth Sarrayins that fel wore   *Saracens; fierce in battle*
To Jerusalem thai com ful yore   *quickly*
To rob and reve with pride.   *plunder; ferocity*
595   And we toke our ost anon   *army*
Ogaines hem we gun gon
Bateyl of hem to abide;
The acountre of hem was so strong   *Their attack*
That mani dyed ther among
600   Or we wald rest that tide.   *Before we could*

"Thurth mi fiftene sone   *sons*
Were the geauntes overcome   *wicked men*
And driven doun to grounde.
Fiftene amirals ther wer nome,   *amirs (commanders); taken*
605   The king gan fle with alle his trome   *troops*
For drede of ous that stounde.   *fear; time*
Ich and mi sones withouten lesing   *lying*
Out of that lond we driven the king
And his men gaf dedli wounde.
610   The king him hight Triamour,   *was called*
A lord he was of gret honour
And man of michel mounde.   *great prowess*

	"Than dede we wel gret foly:	
	We suwed him with maistrie	*followed; with power*
615	Into his owhen lond.	
	Into Alisaundre thai fleye owy,	*Alexandria*
	The cuntré ros up with a cri	
	To help her king an hond.	*their; nearby*
	In a brom feld ther wer hidde	*field full of broom*
620	Thre hundred Sarrayins wele yschridde	*well armed*
	With helme and grimly brond,	*[Each] with helmet; deadly sword*
	Out of that brom thai lepen anon	*sprang*
	And bilapped ous everichon	*surrounded*
	And drof ous alle to schond.	*shameful defeat*
625	"Thai hewen at ous with michel hete	*struck; anger*
	And we layd on hem dintes grete	*blows*
	And slouwen of her ferred,	*struck; troops*
	And ar that we were alle ynome	*before; taken*
	Mani of hem were overcome	
630	Ded wounded under wede.	*Mortally; clothing (armor)*
	Thai were to mani and we to fewe,	*too many*
	Al our armour thai tohewe	*cut to pieces*
	And stiked under ous our stede;	
	Yete we foughten afot long[1]	
635	Til swerdes brosten that were strong	*broke*
	And than yeld we ous for nede.	*surrendered; of necessity*
	"To the king we yolden ous al and some	*submitted; everyone*
	That we might to raunsoun come	
	To save our lives ichon,	
640	Into Alisaunder he ladde ous tho	*led us then*
	And into his prisoun dede ous do,	
	Was maked of lime and ston.	*stone masonry*
	Litel was our drink and lasse our mete,	*food*
	For hunger we wende our lives lete;	*expected to die*
645	Wel wo was ous bigon.	*We were overcome with grief*

---

[1] Lines 633–34: *And stabbed our horses to death under us; / Nevertheless we fought on foot for a long time*

So were we ther alle that yer
With michel sorwe bothe yfere   *all together*
That socour com ous non.   *military assistance*

"So it bifel that riche Soudan   *Sultan*
650   Made a fest of mani a man   *feast for*
Of thritti kinges bi tale.   *by count*
King Triamour com to court tho
And Fabour his sone dede also
With knightes mani and fale   *numerous*
655   The thridde day of that fest   *[On] the third*
That was so riche and so honest   *sumptuous*
So derlich dight in sale.   *richly prepared; hall*
After that fest that riche was
Ther bifel a wonder cas   *astonishing event*
660   Wherthurth ros michel bale.   *misery*

"That riche Soudan hadde a sone
That was yhold a douhti gome,   *regarded; honorable man*
Sadok was his name.
The kinges sone Fabour he cleped him to,   *called to him*
665   Into his chaumber thai gun go,
Tho knightes bothe ysame.   *together*
Sadok gan to Fabour sayn   *ask*
Yif he wald ate ches playn   *chess*
And held ogain him game,   *challenged him to a game*
670   And he answerd in gode maner
He wald play with him yfere   *together*
Withouten ani blame.   *Respectfully (without giving offense)*

"Ate ches thai sett hem to playn,   *At the chessboard*
Tho hendy knightes bothe tuayn
675   That egre were of sight.   *spirited; to see (in appearance)*
Er thai hadde don half a game
With strong wretthe thai gan to grame,   *became infuriated*
Tho gomes michel of might.   *Those men*
Thurth a chek Fabour seyd for soth   *[call of] check*
680   Sadok in hert wex wroth   *became enraged*
And missayd him anonright   *insulted*

40

	And clepd him *fiz a putayn*	*"son of a whore"*
	And smot him with might and main	*vigor*
	Wherthurth ros michel fight.	*great fighting*
685	"With a roke he brac his heved than	*rook (chesspiece); head*
	That the blod biforn out span	*spurted out*
	In that ich place.	*everywhere*
	'Sadok,' seyd than Fabour,	
	'Thou dost me gret deshonour	
690	That thou me manace.	*threaten*
	Nar thou mi lordes sone were	*Were you not*
	Thou schuldest dye right now here.	
	Schustow never hennes passe.'	*You should never leave*
	Sadok stirt up to Fabour	*charged*
695	And cleped him anon, 'Vile traitour!'	
	And smot him in the face.	*hit*
	"With his fest he smot him thore	*fist*
	That Fabour was agreved sore	*[So] that*
	And stirt up in that stounde.	*leaped up immediately*
700	The cheker he hent up fot-hot	*chessboard; picked up suddenly*
	And Sadok in the heved he smot	*on*
	That he fel ded to grounde.	
	His fader sone he hath yteld	
	That he hath the Soudan sone aqueld	*Sultan's son killed*
705	And goven him dethes wounde,	*a fatal wound*
	On hors thai lopen than bilive	*horses; leaped without delay*
	Out of the lond thai gun drive	*dash away*
	For ferd thai were yfounde.	*In fear*
	"When it was the Soudan teld	
710	That his sone was aqueld	*slain*
	And brought of his liif dawe	*deprived of his life*
	On al maner he him bithought	
	Hou that he him wreke mought	*avenge might*
	Thurth jugement of lawe.	
715	After the king he sent an heyghe	*hastily*
	To defende him of that felonie	
	That he his sone hath yslawe	

41

	And bot he wald com anon	*unless*
	With strengthe he schuld on him gon,	*Forceably; punish him*
720	With wilde hors don him drawe.	*cause him to be drawn*

"King Triamour com to court tho
And Fabour his sone dede also
To the Soudans parlement.
When thai biforn him comen beth
725 Thai were adouted of her deth
Her lives thai wende have spent
For the Soudan cleped hem fot-hot
And his sones deth hem atwot
And seyd thai were alle schent;
730 Bot thai hem therof were might
In strong perile he schuld hem dight
And to her jugement.[1]

725		*afraid*
		believed; finished
		called them immediately
		attributed to them
		condemned

"Than dede he com forth a Sarrayine —
Have he Cristes curs and mine
735 With boke and eke with belle —
Out of Egypt he was ycome,
Michel and griselich was that gome
With ani god man to duelle.
He is so michel and unrede
740 Of his sight a man may drede
With tong as Y thee telle;
As blac he is as brodes brend,
He semes as it were a fende
That comen were out of helle.

		he made come forward; Saracen
		Huge; ugly; man
		huge; monstrous
		burnt nails
		devil

745 "For he is so michel of bodi ypight
Ogains him tuelve men have no might
Ben thai never so strong,
For he is four fot sikerly
More than ani man stont him bi,

		well-built
		extremely
		with certainty
		[who] stands; beside

---

[1] Lines 730–32: *Unless they were able to defend themselves / He would condemn them to great danger / And to their punishment*

750	So wonderliche he is long.	*extraordinarily tall*
	Yif King Triamour that ther was	
	Might fenden him in playn place	*defend himself; plateau used for tournaments*
	Of that michel wrong	*great injustice*
	Than is that vile glotoun	*wretch*
755	Made the Soudans champioun	
	Batayl of him to fong.	*undertake*

	"King Triamour answerd than	
	To that riche Soudan	
	In that ich stounde	*same moment*
760	That he wald defende him wele ynough	
	That he never his sone slough	
	No gaf him dedli wounde.	*Nor*
	When he seye Amoraunt so grim —	*monstrous*
	Ther durst no man fight with him	
765	So grille he was on grounde —	*fierce*
	Than asked he respite til a day	*extension of time; for*
	To finde another yif he may	
	Ogaines him durst founde.	*Who would dare to fight against him*

	"Than hadde he respite al that yere	
770	And fourti days so was the maner	*as; custom*
	Thurth lawe was than in lond;	*According to law*
	Yif himselven durst nought fight	
	Finde another yif he might	*is able*
	Ogaines him durst stond.	
775	The king as swithe hom is went,	*quickly*
	Over alle his lond anon he sent	
	After erl, baroun, and bond	
	And asked yif ani wer so bold —	
	Thriddendel his lond have he schold —	*One-third*
780	The batayl durst take an hond.	*accept*

	"Ac for nought that he hot might	*But; might promise*
	Ther was non durst take the fight	
	With the geaunt for his sake.	
	Than was ich out of prisoun nome,	*I; taken*
785	Biforn him he dede me come	

Conseyl of me to take
And asked me at worde fewe
Yif Y wist other Y knewe   *was aware of or knew*
A man so mighti of strake   *mighty of stroke [i.e., strong in battle]*
790 That for him durst take the fight;
Were he burjays other knight   *burgess or*
Riche prince he wald him make.

"And yif Y might ani fende   *find*
He wald make me riche and al mi kende   *kin*
795 And gif me gret honour   *give*
And wold sese into min hond   *transfer by deed*
To helden thriddendel his lond   *possess a third part*
With cité, toun, and tour.
Ac ichim answerd than   *But I him*
800 In alle this warld was ther no man
To fight with that traitour
Bot yif it Gii of Warwike were
Or Herhaud of Ardern his fere   *companion*
In warld thai bere the flour.   *they are the best*

805 "When the king herd tho   *then*
That Y spac of tho knightes to   *What; those*
Ful blithe he was of chere,   *mood*
He kist me so glad he was.
'Merci,' he seyd, 'Erl Jonas;
810 Thou art me leve and dere.   *[to] me dear; precious*
Yif ich hadde here Sir Gii
Or Herhaud that is so hardi
Of the maistri siker Y were.   *victory; certain*
And thou mightest bring me her on   *here one [of them]*
815 Thee and thine sones Y schal lete gon
Fram prisoun quite and skere.'   *exempt; blameless*

"Bi mi lay he dede me swere   *On my faith*
That Y schuld trewelich bode bere   *message*
To tho knightes so hende
820 And seyd to me as swithe anon   *straight after*
With michel sorwe he schuld me slon   *great pain*

	Bot ichem might fende	Unless I am able to find them
	And al mine sones do todrawe;	tear apart (draw)
	And ichim graunt in that thrawe	time
825	To bring hem out of bende.	bondage
	Out of this lond Y went tho	
	With michel care and michel wo;	
	Y nist wider to wende.	knew not; go

	"Y sought hem into the lond of Coyne,	Konya (Iconium)
830	Into Calaber and into Sessoyne,	Calabria; Saxony
	And fro thennes into Almayne,	Germany
	In Tuskan and in Lombardye,	
	In Fraunce and in Normondye,	
	Into the lond of Speyne,	
835	In Braban, in Poil and in Bars,	Apulia; Barbary?
	And into kinges lond of Tars	
	And thurth al Aquitayne,	
	In Cisil, in Hungri and in Ragoun,	Sicily; Ragusa
	In Romayne, Borgoine, and Gastoine	Romania; Burgundy; Gascony
840	And thurthout al Breteyne.	Brittany

	"And into Inglond wenden Y gan	
	And asked ther mani a man	
	Bothe yong and old,	
	And in Warwike that cité	
845	Ther he was lord of that cuntré	(i.e., Guy)
	For to haven in wold.	hold; rule
	Ac Y no fond non lite no miche	But; nobody at all
	That couthe telle me sikerliche	could; certainly
	Of tho to knightes bold,	those two
850	Wher Y schold Gii no Herhaud fende	or
	In no lond fer no hende;	
	Therfore min hert is cold.	dismal

	"For ich have the king mi trewthe yplight	promise sworn
	That Y schal bring Gii now right	right away
855	Yif he olives be.	is alive
	And yive Y bring him nought anon	if
	Wele ich wot he wil me slon —	slay

Therfore wel wo is me —   *distressed*
And min sones he schal don hong   *cause to be hanged*
860 And todrawe with michel wrong,   *pulled to pieces; great injustice*
Tho knightes hende and fre.   *Those*
And yif thai dye gret harm it is   *a matter for great sorrow*
For hem ich have swiche sorwe, ywis,   *such; truly*
Mine hert wil breken on thre."   *into three parts*

865 "God man," seyd Gii, "listen me now,
For thine sones gret sorwe hastow
And no wonder it nis   *it is no wonder [at all]*
When thou Gii and Herhaud hath sought
And thou no may hem finde nought;
870 Thi care is michel, ywis.
Thurth hem thine hope was to go fre
And thi sones al forth with thee
Thurth Godes help and his.
Sum time bi dayes old
875 For douhti men thai wer told   *said to be*
And holden of gret priis.   *held in high esteem*

"Thurth Godes helpe our Dright —   *our Lord*
He be min help and give me might
And leve me wele to spede —
880 And for Gyes love and Herhaud also
That thou hast sought with michel wo,
That douhti were of dede,
Batayl ichil now for thee fong   *undertake*
Ogain the geaunt that is so strong,   *Against*
885 Thou seyst is so unrede.   *savage (fierce)*
And thei he be the fende outright   *Even if he is the devil himself*
Y schal for thee take the fight
And help thee at this nede."   *in this time of peril*

When th'erl herd him speke so
890 That he wald batayl fong for him tho   *undertake*
He biheld fot and heved.   *scrutinized [Guy from] head to toe*
Michel he was of bodi pight,   *Large; built*
A man he semed of michel might

46

	Ac pouerliche he was biweved.	*poorly; clothed*
895	With a long berd his neb was growe,	*face*
	Miche wo him thought he hadde ydrowe.	*hardship; overcome*
	He wende his wit were reved	*suspected; lost his mind*
	For he seyd he wald as yern	*immediately*
	Fight with that geaunt stern	
900	Bot yif he hadde him preved.	*Unless; denied*

	"God man," than seyd he,	
	"God almighten foryeld it thee	*[May] God Almighty for this reward you*
	That is so michel of might	*Who are*
	Thatow wost batayl for me fong	*That you would; undertake*
905	Ogain the geaunt that is so strong;	
	Thou knowest him nought, Y plight,	*I swear*
	For yif he loked on thee with wrake,	*vengefulness*
	Sternliche with his eyghen blake,	*black eyes*
	So grim he is of sight	*terrifying; to see*
910	Wastow never so bold in al thi teime	*time*
	Thatow durst batayl of him nim	*take*
	No hold ogaines him fight."	

	"Gode man," seyd Gii, "lat be that thought	
	For swiche wordes help ous nought	*such*
915	Ogain that schrewe qued.	*wicked devil*
	Mani hath loked me opon	
	With wicked wil, mani on	
	That wald han had min hed,	
	And thei no fled Y never yete	
920	No never for ferd batayl lete,	
	For no man that brac bred.[1]	
	And thei he be the devels rote	*though; offspring*
	Y schal nought fle him afot,	*on foot*
	Bi Him that suffred ded."	*death*

---

[1] Lines 919–21: *And despite them, I have never yet fled / Nor ever left a battle out of fear, / Not for any man (lit., for no man that ever broke bread)*

47

925	"Leve sir," than seyd he,	
	"God of heven foryeld it te.	*reward you for it*
	Thine wordes er ful swete."	*are very pleasing*
	For joie he hadde in hert that stounde;	*moment*
	On knes he fel adoun to grounde	
930	And kist Sir Gyes fet.	
	Gii tok him up in armes to,	
	Into Alisaunder thai gun go	
	With the king to mete.	
	And when thai com into the tour	
935	Bifor the king Sir Triamour	
	Wel fair thai gun him grete.	*courteously*

	And when he seye th'erl Jonas	
	Unnethe he knewe him in the fas	*Hardly; face*
	So chaunged was his ble.	*expression (countenance)*
940	"Erl Jonas," seyd the king,	
	"Telle me now withouten lesing	
	Gii and Herhaud where ben he?"	*they*
	Th'erl answerd and siked sore,	*sighed sadly*
	"Gii no Herhaud sestow no more	*you [will] see*
945	For sothe Y telle thee.	
	For hem ich have in Inglond ben	
	And Y no might hem nowhar sen,	
	Therfore wel wo is me.	

	"Ac the lond folk teld me in speche	*people of that country*
950	That Gii was gon halwen to seche	*shrines; seek*
	Wel fer in uncouthe lond	*unknown*
	And Herhaud after him is went	
	For to seche him verrament.	*truly*
	Noither of hem Y no fond.	
955	Ac this man ich have brought to thee	
	That hath ben man of gret bounté	*prowess*
	That wele dar take on hond	*undertake*
	Ogain the geaunt that is so fel	*fierce*
	Al for to fende thee ful wel	*defend*
960	For drede wil he nought wond."	*fear; hesitate*

48

"Erl Jonas," seyd the king,
"Loke with him be no feynting[1]
That Y deseyved be.
And yif ther be thou schalt anon
965   Be honged and thi sones ichon."
"Y graunt, sir," than seyd he.   *I give my assurance*
The king cleped Sir Gyoun
And asked him at schort resoun,   *in short*
"What is thi name tel me?"
970   Sir Gii answerd to the king,
"Youn," he seyd, "withouten lesing   *lying*
Men clepeth me in mi cuntré."

"What cuntré artow?" the king sede.
"Of Inglond, so God me rede;   *counsel*
975   Therin ich was yborn."
"O we," seyd the king, "artow Inglis knight?   *Oh!; English*
Than schuld Y thurth skil and right   *by reason and by rights*
Hate thee ever more.
Knewe thou nought the gode Gii
980   Or Herhaud that was so hardi?
Tel me the sothe bifore.   *to my face*
Wele ought ich be Gyes fo man;   *personal enemy*
He slough mi brother Helmadan,
Thurth him icham forlore.   *deprived*

985   "Min em he slough, the riche Soudan,   *uncle*
Ate mete among ous everilkan.   *At table; us all (every each one)*
Seyghe Y never man so bigin.   *Saw; act*
Y seyghe hou he his heved of smot   *head cut off*
And bar it oway with him fot-hot   *quickly*
990   Maugré that was therinne.   *Disgrace there was in that act*
After him we driven tho —   *chased then*
The devel halp him thennes to go,
Y trowe he is of his kinne.   *believe; (i.e., the devil's)*
Mahoun gaf that thou wer he,   *Muhammad grant*

---

[1] *Be on your guard against any cowardliness in him*

995	Ful siker might Y than be	*certain*
	The maistri forto winne."	*victory*

Sir Gii answerd to the king,
"Wel wele Y knowe withouten lesing   *Very well; lying*
Herhaud so God me rede
1000 And yif thou haddest her on here   *one of them here*
Of the maistri siker thou were
The bateyl forto bede."   *command*
The king asked him anonright,   *immediately*
"Whi artow thus ivel ydight   *inadequately equipped*
1005 And in thus pouer wede?   *poor raiment*
A feble lord thou servest, so thenketh me,
Or oway he hath driven thee
For sum ivel dede."[1]

"Nay, sir, for God," quath Gii,
1010 "A wel gode Lord than serve Y.
With Him was no blame.   *fault*
Wel michel honour He me dede
And gret worthschipe in everi stede   *everywhere*
And sore ich have Him grame;   *troubled (vexed)*
1015 And therfore icham thus ydight   *dressed*
To cri Him merci day and night   *beg [to] Him [for]*
Til we ben frendes same.   *together*
And mi Lord and Y frende be   *When; friends*
Ichil wende hom to mi cuntré   *return*
1020 And live with joie and game."   *pleasure*

"Frende Youn," seyd the king,
"Wiltow fight for mi thing   *sake*
Other Y schal another purvay?"   *Or*
"Therfor com ich hider," quath Gii,
1025 "Thurth Godes help and our Levedi
As wele as Y may.

[1] Lines 1006–08: *You serve an inferior lord, it seems to me, / [Either that] or he has exiled you / Because of some terrible crime*

	Bot first th'erl Jonas and his sones	
	Schal be deliverd out of prisones	
	This ich selve day."	*today*
1030	The king answerd, "Y graunt thee.	
	Mahoun he mot thine help be	*Muhammed; may*
	That is mi lord verray."	*in truth*
	"Nay," seyd Gii, "bot Marie sone	*only Mary's son*
	He mot to help come	
1035	For Mahoun is worth nought."	*nothing*
	"Frende Youn," seyd the king,	
	"Understond now mi teling,	
	Al what ich have ythought	*Everything*
	Yif that thou may overcom the fight	*are able to win*
1040	And defende me with right	*with justice*
	The wrong is on me sought,	*injustice; done against me*
	So michel Y schal for thee do	
	That men schal speke therof evermo	*evermore*
	As wide as this warld is wrought.	*Throughout the world*
1045	"Alle the men that in my prisoun be	
	Thai schul be deliverd for love of thee	
	That Cristen men be told.[1]	
	Fram henne to Ynde that cité	*here; India*
	Quite-claym thai schul go fre	*[By] deed of release*
1050	Bothe yong and old.	
	And so gode pes Y schal festen anon	*such peaceful relations; establish*
	That Cristen men schul comen and gon	
	To her owhen wille in wold."	*world*
	"Gramerci," than seyd Sir Gii,	
1055	"That is a fair gift sikerly,	*promise certainly*
	God leve thee it wele to hold."	*[May] God help you to grant it*
	The king dede make a bathe anonright	*bath*
	For to bathe Gii and better dight;	*dress him*

---

[1] Lines 1045–47: *All men in my prison that are counted Christian shall be released out of respect for you*

51

	In silk he wald him schrede.	*clothe*
1060	"Nay, sir," than seyd Sir Gii,	
	"Swiche clothes non kepe Y	*Such; I do not wish for*
	Also God me rede	
	To were clothes gold bigo	*wear; gold-embroidered*
	For Y was never wont therto	*it was never my desire*
1065	No non so worthliche wede.	*fine clothes*
	Mete and drink anough give me	*food; sufficient*
	And riche clothes lat thou be,	
	Y kepe non swiche prede."	*I do not care about such ostentation*

	And when the time com to th'ende	
1070	That thai schuld to court wende	
	Ther sembled a fair ferred.	*company of people*
	King Triamour maked him yare tho	*ready*
	And Fabour his sone dede also	
	With knightes stithe on stede.	*strong; horse*
1075	To courtward than went he	*they*
	To Espire that riche cité	*Spires*
	With joie and michel prede.	*display*
	To the Soudan thai went on heye	*in haste*
	With wel gret chevalrie	*host of mounted knights*
1080	Bateyle forto bede.	*offer*

	Gii was ful wele in armes dight	
	With helme and plate and brini bright	*helmet; plate armor; coat of mail*
	The best that ever ware.	
	The hauberk he hadde was Renis	*Rhenish (from the region of the Rhine river)*
1085	That was King Clarels, ywis,	*truly*
	In Jerusalem when he was thare.	
	A thef stale it in that stede	*place*
	And oway therwith him dede,	
	To hethenesse he it bare,	*Muslim lands*
1090	King Triamours elders it bought	*ancestors*
	And in her hord-house thai thought	*their treasure house*
	To hold it ever mare.	

	Sir Gii thai toke it in that plas.	
	Thritti winter afrayd it nas;	*disturbed; was not*

1095	Ful clere it was of mayle	*gleaming*
	As bright as ani silver it was,	
	The halle schon therof as sonne of glas	*sun; glass*
	For sothe withouten fayle.	*Truly without doubt*
	His helme was of so michel might	
1100	Was never man overcomen in fight	
	That hadde it on his ventayle.	*face plate*
	It was Alisaunders the gret lording	
	When he faught with Poreus the king	
	That hard him gan aseyle.	*assail*

1105	A gode swerd he hadde withouten faile	*without doubt*
	That was Ectors in Troye batayle,	
	In gest as-so men fint.	*story; find*
	Ar he that swerd dede forgon	*Before; give up*
	Of Grece he slough ther mani on	
1110	That died thurth that dint.	*blow*
	Hose and gambisoun so gode knight schold,	*leg guards; jacket; as*
	A targe listed with gold	*shield bordered*
	About his swere he hint.	*neck; carried*
	Nas never wepen that ever was make	
1115	That o schel might therof take	
	Namore than of the flint.[1]	

	For King Triamours elders it laught,	*obtained it*
	King Darri sum time it aught,	*owned*
	That Gii was under pight.	*protected by*
1120	Ich man axe other bigan	*ask*
	Whennes and who was that man	*From where*
	That with the geaunt durst fight.	*dared*
	King Triamour seyd with wordes fre	
	"Sir Soudan, herken now to me	*listen*
1125	Astow art hendy knight.	
	To thi court icham now come	

---

[1] Lines 1114–16: *No weapon had ever been made / That could pierce that shield / Anymore than [it could pierce] a piece of flint*

To defende me of that ich gome   *myself; same man*
That is so stern of sight.   *dreadful to look at*

"This litel knight that stont me by   *stands*
1130   Schal fende me of that felonie   *defend; crime*
And make me quite and skere."   *exonerated of misdoing*
"Be stille," seyd the Soudan tho,   *silent*
"That batail schal wel sone be go   *begin immediately*
Also brouke Y mi swere!"   *On my life! (lit., as I break my neck)*
1135   He dede clepe Amorant so grim   *call; ugly*
And Gii stode and loked on him
Hou foule he was of chere.   *appearance*
"It is," seyd Gii, "no mannes sone,
It is a devel fram helle is come,
1140   What wonder doth he here?   *evil*

"Who might his dintes dreye   *endure*
That he no schuld dye an heye   *quickly*
So strong he is of dede?"
Than speken thai alle of the batayle,   *discussed together*
1145   Where it schuld be withouten fayle
Thai token hem to rede.   *confer*
Than loked thai it schuld be   *decided*
In a launde under the cité;   *plain; beside*
Thider thai gun hem lede.
1150   With a river it ern al about,   *was surrounded*
Therin schuld fight tho knightes stout;
Thai might fle for no nede.[1]

Over the water thai went in a bot,
On hors thai lopen fot-hot   *leaped*
1155   Tho knightes egre of mode.   *spirit*
Thai priked the stedes that thai on sete   *spurred on*
And smiten togider with dentes grete   *blows*
And ferd as thai wer wode   *behaved; berserk*
Til her schaftes in that tide   *their lances*

---

[1] *They would not be able to flee [the battlefield] under any circumstances*

1160	Gun to schiver bi ich a side	*shatter; all around*
	About hem ther thai stode.	
	Than thai drough her swerdes grounde	*drew; whetted*
	And hewe togider with grimli wounde	
	Til thai spradde al ablode.	*were covered all over with blood*
1165	Sir Amoraunt drough his gode brond	
	That wele carf al that it fond	*easily cut; met with*
	When he hadde lorn his launce.	*lost*
	That never armour might withstond	
	That was made of smitthes hond	
1170	In hethenesse no in Fraunce.[1]	
	It was Sir Ercules the strong	*had belonged to*
	That mani he slough therwith with wrong	*wickedness*
	In batayle and in destaunce.	*armed warfare*
	Ther was never man that it bere	
1175	Overcomen in batayle no in were	
	Bot it were thurth meschaunce.[2]	
	It was bathed in the flom of Helle,	*river of Hell*
	Agnes gaf it him to wille	*wield*
	He schuld the better spede.	
1180	Who that bar that swerd of might	
	Was never man overcomen in fight	*beaten by another man*
	Bot it were thurth unlede.	*Unless; through treachery*
	Ther worth Sir Gii to deth ybrought	*There Sir Guy would have died*
	Bot yif God have of him thought,	*Unless*
1185	His best help at nede.	
	Togider thai wer yern heweinde	*vigorously striking*
	With her brondes wele kerveinde	*their very sharp swords*
	And maden her sides blede.	

---

[1] Lines 1168–70: *No armor exists (lit., no armor made by a smith), either in Muslim lands or in France, which would be able to withstand it*

[2] Lines 1174–76: *No man that had ever carried it / Had been defeated in battle or in war / Except through treachery*

Sir Amoraunt was agreved in hert
1190 And smot to Gii a dint ful smert
With alle the might he gan welde
And hitt him on the helme so bright
That alle the stones of michel might   *precious stones*
Fleyghe doun in the feld.   *Fell on the ground*
1195 Al of the helme the swerd out stint   *struck*
And forth right with that selve dint   *same blow*
Other half fot of the scheld   *One and a half foot*
That never was atamed ar than   *pierced before*
For knight no for no nother man   *By*
1200 No were he never so beld.   *however powerful*

The sadelbowe he clef atuo,   *split in two*
The stedes nek he dede also
With his grimli brond;
Withouten wem or ani wounde   *injury*
1205 Wele half a fot into the grounde   *At least*
The scharp swerd it wond.   *thrust down*
Sir Gii to grounde fallen is,
He stirt up anon, ywis,   *jumped up*
And loked and gan withstond.   *stood firm*
1210 Anon right in that ich stede   *very place*
To God almighten he bad his bede   *said his prayer*
And held up bothe his hond.   *hands*

Sir Gii anon up stirt
As man that was agremed in hert;   *incensed*
1215 Nought wel long he lay.   *Not for very long*
"Lord," seyd Gii, "God Almight
That made the therkenes to the night   *darkness into*
So help me today.
Scheld me fro this geaunt strong
1220 That Y no deth of him afong   *receive*
Astow art lord verray.   *truly*
That dint," he seyd, "was ivel sett   *said [to Amorant]; poorly struck*
Wele schal Y com out of thi dett,   *repay you your debt (i.e., with a return blow)*
Yif that Y libbe may."   *live*

1225	Gii hent his swerd that was ful kene	*seized*
	And smot Amoraunt with hert tene	*angry*
	A dint that sat ful sore	
	That a quarter of his scheld	
	He made to fleye in the feld	*fall to the ground*
1230	Al with his grimli gore.	*deadly sword*
	The stedes nek he smot atuo,	
	Amoraunt to grounde is fallen tho,	
	Wo was him therfore.	*Distressed*
	Than were on fot tho knightes bold,	*those*
1235	Fight o fot yif thai wold —	*on*
	Her stedes thai han forlore.	*lost*
	Amoraunt with hert ful grim	*fierce*
	Smot to Gii, and Gii to him	
	With strokes stern and stive.	*merciless and unflinching*
1240	Hard thai hewe with swerdes clere	*[So] hard; gleaming*
	That helme and swerd that strong were	
	Thai gun hem al todrive.	*break to pieces*
	Hard foughten tho champiouns	*[So] hard*
	That bothe plates and hauberjouns	*plates of armor; coats of mail*
1245	Thai gun to ret and rive;	*split; crack*
	And laiden on with dintes gret	
	Aither of hem so other gan bete	
	That wo was hem olive.	
	Sir Amoraunt was agreved strong	*severely annoyed*
1250	That o man stode him tho so long,	*one; withstood; then*
	To Gii a strok he raught	*reached*
	And hit him on the helme so bright	
	That al the floures fel doun right	*ornamental flowers*
	With a ful grimly draught.	*very fierce blow*
1255	The cercle of gold he carf ato	*carved in two*
	And forth with his dint also,	
	Ther bileved it nought.[1]	
	On the scheld the swerd doun fel	

---

[1] Lines 1256–57: *And continued forward with his stroke, / It did not stop there*

And cleve it into halvendel;   *in half*
1260 Almost to grounde him brought.

What with the swerdes out draweing,
And with his hetelich out braiding[1]
Ther fel a wonder cas.   *occurred an extraordinary happening*
Sir Gii fel on knes to grounde
1265 And stirt up in that selve stounde   *same moment*
And seyd, "Lord, ful of grace,
Never dint of knight non
No might me are knele don[2]
In no stede ther Y was."   *place where*
1270 Sir Gii hent up his swerd fot-hot,   *lifted up*
Amoraunt on the hod he smot   *hood [of mail]*
That he stumbled in the place.   *[So] that*

He hit him on the helme an heyghe   *at once*
And with that dint the swerd it fleyghe,   *moved swiftly*
1275 Bi the nasel it gan doun founde   *nose-guard; proceeded*
And so it dede bi the ventayle   *face-guard*
And carf it ato saunfaile   *with no doubt*
And into his flesche a wounde.
His targe with gold list   *shield; rim*
1280 He carf atuo thurth help of Crist   *in two*
He cleve that ich stounde.   *cleaved; same instant*
So heteliche the brond out he plight   *fiercely; drew*
That Amorant anonright
Fel on knes to grounde.

1285 So strong batayle was hem bituene,
So seyd thai that might it sene,
That seye thai never non swiche;
That never was of wiman born

---

[1] Lines 1261–62: *What with pulling out the sword, / And fiercely disengaging it*

[2] Lines 1267–68: *Never before has the blow of any knight forced me to kneel down*

Swiche to knightes as thai worn [1]
1290   That foughten togider with wreche   *vengeful wrath*
On a day bifor the nativité
Of Seyn Jon the martir fre
That holy man is to seche.   *to appeal to*
Togider fought tho barouns bothe   *warriors*
1295   That in hert wer so wrothe,
Of love was ther no speche.

Sir Amoraunt withdrough him   *himself*
With loureand chere wroth and grim,   *scowling face*
For the blod of him was lete,
1300   That drink he most other his liif forgon   *or; lose*
So strong thrust yede him opon   *thirst was upon him*
So michel was his hete.   *thirst*
"Fourti batayls ichave overcome
Ac fond Y never er moder sone   *before [any] mother's son*
1305   That me so sore gan bete.
Tel me," he seyd, "what artow?   *what [manner of man] are you*
Felt Y never man ar now   *before*
That gaf dintes so grete.

"Tel me," he seyd, "wennes thou be?   *from which place*
1310   For thou art strong, so mot Y the,   *so may I thrive*
And of michel might."
Sir Gii answerd withouten bost,   *without arrogance (meekly)*
"Cristen icham wele thou wost   *know*
Of Inglond born, Y plight.   *I assure you*
1315   King Triamour me hider brought
For to defenden him yif Y mought   *am able*
Of that michel unright   *great injustice*
That ye beren on him with wough   *with injustice*
That Fabour never Sadony slough
1320   Noither bi day no night."

---

[1] Lines 1285–89: *Such a violent battle arose between them, / So those who watched it said, / That they had never seen such [a fight] / And that there never were of woman born / Two such knights as they were*

"O artow Inglis?" seyd Amorant.
"Now wald mi lord Ternagaunt   *may Termagant bring it about*
That thou were Gii the strong.
Mahoun gaf that thou wer he,   *grant*
1325   Blithe wald Y than be
Batail of him to fong;   *undertake*
For he hath destrud al our lawe   *faith (religion)*
His heved wald ichave ful fawe   *head; very gladly*
Or heighe on galwes hong;
1330   For kever schal we never er more   *recover; never again*
That he hath don ous forlore   *That which he has caused us to lose*
With wel michel wrong.

"With michel wrong and michel wough
Fourti thousend of ous he slough   *killed*
1335   In Costentin on a day.   *Constantinople*
He and Herhaud his felawe   *comrade*
Michel han destrud our lawe   *religion*
That ever more mon Y may.   *lament*
Yif he wer slain with brond of stiel
1340   Than were Y wroken on him ful wel   *avenged*
That han destrud our lay."   *religion*
Sir Gii answerd, "Whi seistow so?   *say you*
Hath Gii ani thing thee misdo?"   *done you any personal harm*
Amoraunt seyd, "Nay,

1345   "Ac it wer gret worthschip, ywis,   *But; honor*
To alle the folk of hethenisse   *non-Christian lands*
That Y hadde so wroken mi kende.   *avenged my people*
Cristen," he seyd, "listen to me,
The weder is hot astow may se,
1350   Y pray thee, leve frende,   *dear*
Leve to drink thou lat me gon   *Permission*
For the lordes love thou levest on,   *believe*
Astow art gode and hende.
For thrist mi hert wil tospring   *thirst; burst apart*
1355   And for hete withouten lesing
Mi live wil fro me wende.   *life*

"And yif Y schal be thus aqueld   *killed*
Thurth strong hete in the feld   *battlefield*
It were ogain thee skille.   *against your better judgement*
1360   Unworthschipe it war to thee —   *Dishonorable*
It were thee gret vileté   *to you; shame*
In wat lond thou com tille.   *whatever; to*
Ac lete me drink a litel wight   *small amount*
For thi lordes love ful of might
1365   That thou lovest with wille   *whole-heartedly*
And Y thee hot bi mi lay   *I assure you; faith*
Yif thou have ani threst today
Thou shalt drink al thi fille."

Sir Gii answerd, "Y graunt thee
1370   And yete today thou yeld it me[1]
Withouten ani fayle."
And when he hadde leve of Sir Gii   *permission from*
He was ful glad sikerli,
No lenger nold he dayle.   *delay*
1375   To the river ful swithe he ran,   *quickly*
His helme of his heved he nam   *off; took*
And unlaced his ventayle.   *face-piece*
When he hadde dronken alle his fille
He stirt up with hert grille   *fierce*
1380   And Sir Gii he gan to asayle.   *attack*

"Knight," he seyd, "yeld thee bilive   *surrender yourself immediately*
For thou art giled, so mot Y thrive.   *beguiled*
Now ichave a drink
Icham as fresche as ich was amorwe.   *in the morning*
1385   Thou schalt dye with michel sorwe
For sothe withouten lesing."
Than thai drowen her swerdes long
Tho knightes that wer stern and strong
Withouten more dueling   *delay*
1390   And aither gan other ther asayle

---

[1] *Provided that you return [the favor] to me today*

61

And ther bigan a strong bataile
With wel strong fighting.

Amoraunt was ful egre of mode   *enraged*
And smot to Gii as he wer wode —   *as [if]; mad*
1395   Ful egre he was to fight —   *Very impatient*
That a quarter of his scheld   *[So] that*
He made it fleye into the feld
And of his brini bright.   *coat of mail*
Of his scholder the swerd glod doun   *struck*
1400   That bothe plates and hauberjoun   *plate armor; mail*
He carf atuo, Y plight.   *in two, I swear*
Al to the naked hide, ywis,   *skin*
And nought of flesche atamed is   *But; pierced*
Thurth grace of God almight.

1405   The scharp swerd doun gan glide
Fast bi Sir Gyes side —   *Close*
His knew it com ful neye —   *knee; near*
That gambisoun and jambler   *[So] that jacket and leg armor*
Bothe it karf atuo yfere;   *simultaneously*
1410   Into th'erthe the swerd it fleye   *thrust*
Withouten wem or ani wounde   *blemish*
Half a fot into the grounde,
That mani man it seye.   *saw*
And when Gii seye that fair grace   *miracle*
1415   That nothing wounded he was
Jhesu he thanked on heye.

And when Gii feld him so smite   *felt himself struck in this way*
He was wroth ye mow wite;   *may be sure*
To Amoraunt he gan reken   *made his way*
1420   He hent his brond with wel gode wille   *grasped*
And stroke to him with hert grille;   *furious*
His scheld he gan tobreken.   *shattered*
So hetelich Gii him smot   *fiercely*
That into the scholder half a fot
1425   The gode swerd gan reken.   *penetrated*
And with that strok Gii withdrough

62

Weri he was forfoughten ynough,   *with fighting so much*
To Amoraunt he gan speken.

1430
"Sir Amoraunt," than seyd Gii,
"For Godes love now merci
Yif that thi wille be.
Ichave swiche thrist ther Y stond   *where*
Y may unnethe drawe min hond   *hardly*
Therfore wel wo is me.
1435 Yeld me now that ich dede,   *Grant; same favor*
Y gaf thee leve to drink at nede.
Astow art hende and fre,   *courteous; noble*
Leve to drink thou lat me go
As it was covenaunt bituen ous to   *agreed*
1440 For Godes love Y pray thee."

"Hold thi pes," seyd Amoraunt,   *Be silent*
"For bi mi lord Sir Ternagaunt
Leve no hastow non.
Ac now that Y the sothe se
1445 That thou ginnes to feynt thee   *exhaust yourself*
Thine heved thou schalt forgon."   *head*
"Amoraunt," seyd Gii, "do aright,   *act in the right way*
Lete me drink a litel wight   *bit*
As Y dede thee anon   *previously*
1450 And togider fight we;
Who schal be maister we schal se
Wiche of ous may other slon."

"Hold thi pays," seyd Amoraunt,   *peace*
"Y nil nought held thee covenaunt   *keep my promise to you*
1455 For ful this toun of gold,
For when ichave thee sleyn now right
The Soudan treweli hath me hight   *promised*
His lond gif me he schold
Ever more to have and hold fre
1460 And give me his douhter bright o ble,   *fair of face*
The miriest may on mold.   *most beautiful girl on earth*
When ichave thee sleyn this day

He schal give me that fair may
With alle his lond to hold.   *possess*

1465   "Ac do now wele and unarme thee   *yourself*
        And trewelich yeld thou thee to me   *surrender yourself*
        Olive Y lat thee gon.   *Alive*
        And yif thou wilt nought do bi mi red   *advice*
        Thou schalt dye on ivel ded   *suffer a painful death*
1470   Right now Y schal thee slon."
        "Nay," seyd Gii, "that war no lawe.   *punishment*
        Ich hadde lever to ben todrawe   *rather; dismembered*
        Than swiche a dede to don.
        Ar ich wald creaunt yeld me
1475   Ich hadde lever anhanged be
        And brent bothe flesche and bon."[1]

        Than seyd Amoraunt at a word
        "Bi the treuthe thou owe thi lord   *fidelity*
        That thou lovest so dere
1480   Tel me what thi name it be
        And leve to drink give Y thee   *I [will] grant*
        Thi fille of this river.
        Thou seyd thi name is Sir Youn;
        It is nought so bi Seyn Mahoun,   *Saint*
1485   It is a lesing fere.   *complete lie*
        Yif thi name were Youn right   *indeed*
        Thou nere nought of so miche might
        No thus unbiknowen here."[2]

        "Frende," seyd Gii, "Y schal telle thee;
1490   Astow art hendi man and fre
        Thou wray me to no wight.   *reveal my identity to no person*
        Gii of Warwike mi name it is,
        In Inglond Y was born, ywis.

---

[1] Lines 1474–76: *Before I would acknowledge myself defeated / I would rather be hanged / And my body burnt to ashes (lit., both flesh and bone burnt)*

[2] Lines 1487–88: *You could not be of such strength / And remain unheard of here*

Lete me now drink with right."   *rightly (as promised)*
1495 When Amoraunt seye sikerly
      That it was the gode Gii
      That ogaines him was dight   *against; set*
      He loked on him with michel wrake,   *vengefulness*
      Sternliche with his eyghen blake
1500 With an unsemli sight.   *ugly glare*

      "Sir Gii," he seyd, "welcom to me.
      Mahoun, mi lord, Y thank thee
      That ich have thee herinne.
      Michel schame thou hast me don,
1505 Thi liif thou schalt as tite forgon,   *immediately*
      Thi bodi schal atuinne   *[be cut] into two parts*
      And thine heved, bi Ternagant,
      Mi leman schal have to presaunt   *as a gift*
      That comly is of kinne.   *of noble birth*
1510 Hennes forward siker thou be
      Leve no tit thee non of me
      For al this warld to winne."[1]

      "Allas," seyd Gii, "what schal Y don?
      Now Y no may have drink non
1515 Mine hert breketh ato."   *breaks in two*
      Anon he bithought him thenne   *decided to himself*
      Right to the river he most renne;   *must run*
      He turned him and gan to go.
      Amoraunt with swerd on hond   *in*
1520 He thought have driven Gii to schond   *destruction*
      With sorwe he wald him slo.   *pain*
      Gii ran to the water right,   *straight to*
      Bot on him thenke God Almight   *Unless he calls upon*
      Up cometh he never mo.

---

[1] Lines 1510–12: *Hence forward you can be certain / That no permission [to drink] will come to you from me, / Even [if I could thereby] win all of this world*

1525	Tho was Sir Gii in gret drede.	*danger*
	In the water he stode to his girdel stede	*waist*
	And that thought him ful gode.	
	In the water he dept his heved anon	*dipped*
	Over the schulders he dede it gon	
1530	That keled wele his blod.	*cooled; blood*
	And when Gii hadde dronken anough	
	Hetelich his heved up he drough	*Sharply*
	Out of that ich flod	*same*
	And Amoraunt stode opon the lond	
1535	With a drawen swerd in hond	
	And smot Gii ther he stode.	*where*

	Hetelich he smot Gyoun,	*Fiercely*
	Into that water he fel adoun	
	With that dint unride	*violent*
1540	That the water arn him about.	*ran*
	Sir Gii stirt up in gret dout,	*fear*
	For nothing he nold abide,	*would not delay*
	And schoke his heved as knight bold.	
	"In this water icham ful cold	
1545	Wombe, rigge, and side	*Belly, back*
	And no leve, sir, ich hadde of thee	
	And therfore have thou miche maugré	*shame*
	And ivel thee mot bitide."	*bad luck to you*

	Sir Gii stirt up withouten fayl	
1550	And Amoraunt he gan to asayl;	
	To fight he was ful boun.	*eager*
	Hard togider thai gan to fight;	
	Of love was ther no speche, Y plight,	
	Bot heweing with swerdes broun.	*bright*
1555	"Amoraunt," than seyd Gii,	
	"Thou art ful fals sikerly	
	And fulfilt of tresoun.	*full of deceit*
	No more wil Y trust to thee	
	For no bihest thou hotest me.	*promise; make*
1560	Thou art a fals glotoun."	*villain*

	Hard togider thai gun fight	
	Fro the morwe to the night	
	That long somers day.	
	So long thai foughten bothe tho	
1565	Wiche was the better of hem to	
	No man chese no may.	
	Bot at a strok as Amoraunt cast	*extended*
	Sir Gii mett with him in hast	
	And taught him a sori play.	*gave him painful instruction*
1570	The right arme with the swerd fot-hot	
	Bi the scholder of he it smot,	*off*
	To grounde it fleye oway.	
	When Amoraunt feld him so smite	*felt himself thus struck*
	In his left hond with michel hete	*ferocity*
1575	The swerd he hent fot-hot.	*seized quickly*
	As a lyoun than ferd he,	*lion*
	Thritti sautes he made and thre	*Thirty-three attacks*
	With his swerd that wel bot.	*cut*
	Bot for the blod that of him ran	*However; because of*
1580	Amoraunt strengthe slake bigan.	*diminish*
	When Gii that soth wot	*knew the truth (realized)*
	That Amoraunt was faynting	
	Sir Gii him folwed withouten dueling;	*delay*
	That other hond of he smot.	*off*
1585	When Amoraunt had bothe hondes forlore	
	A wreche he held himself therfore;	
	His wit was al todreved.	*mind; afflicted*
	On Sir Gii he lepe with alle his might	*leaped*
	That almast he had feld him doun right,	*knocked him right over*
1590	And Sir Gii was agreved	
	And stirt bisiden fot-hot,	*jumped aside quickly*
	And Amoraunt in the nek he smot.	
	His might he hath him bireved;	*deprived*
	He fel to grounde withouten faile	
1595	And Sir Gii unlaced his ventayle	
	And he strok of his heved.	

67

Over the water he went in a bot
And present therwith fot-hot   *presented [the head] quickly to*
The king Sir Triamour.
1600   The king Sir Triamour than
Went to that riche Soudan
And also his sone Fabour.
Than was the Soudan swithe wo,   *extremely sorrowful*
Quite-claim he lete hem go
1605   With wel michel honour.
Into Alisaunder thai went that cité
And ladde with hem Sir Gii the fre   *noble*
That hadde ben her socour.   *their champion*

The king tok th'erl Jonas tho
1610   And clept him in his armes to   *embraced*
And kist him swete, ich wene,   *affectionately, I believe*
An hundred times and yete mo   *and then more*
And quite-claim he lete him go
And his sones fiftene.
1615   "Erl Jonas," seyd the king,
"Herken now to my teling
And what ichil mene: *I will say*
For mi liif thou savedest me   *Because you saved my life*
Half mi lond ich graunt thee
1620   With this knight strong and kene.

"Understond to me, sir knight,
Mahoun gave ful of might   *grant*
Thou wost duelle with me;
Thridde part mi lond Y give thee to,   *A third of*
1625   Michel honour ichil thee do,
A riche prince make thee.
Y nil nought thou forsake God thine;   *will not [ask that]*
Thou art bileveand wele afine,   *believing perfectly*
Better may no be."
1630   Sir Gii answerd him ful stille: *quietly*
"Sir, of thi lond nought Y nille   *I will have none*
For sothe Y telle thee."

That erl to Jerusalem went anon,
Gii of Warwike with him gan gon
1635 And alle his sones on rawe.   *together*
Th'erl wold yif he might
Wite the name of that knight   *Know*
Yif he him evermore sawe.
"In conseyl, sir knight," than seyd he,   *confidence*
1640 "That thou Youn dost clep thee,   *Though; call yourself*
Thou no hatest nought so Y trowe.   *You are not called that I reckon*
For Jhesu love Y pray thee
That died on the Rode tre   *Cross*
Thi right name be aknawe."   *made known*

1645 Sir Gii seyd, "Thou schalt now here   *hear*
Sethen thou frainest me in this maner;   *Since; ask*
Mi name ichil thee sayn: *I will tell you*
Gii of Warwike mi name is right,   *properly*
Astow art hende and gentil knight
1650 To non thou schalt me wrayn.   *reveal*
Batayl for thi love Y nam   *took*
And the geaunt overcam;
Therof ich am ful fain."   *pleased*
When th'erl seye it was Sir Gii   *saw*
1655 He fel doun on knes him bi
And wepe with both his ayn.   *eyes*

"For Godes love," he seyd, "merci.
Whi artow so pouer Sir Gii
And art of so gret valour?
1660 Here ich give thee in this place
Al th'erldam of Durras
Cité and castel tour.
Thi man ichil bicomen and be   *vassal*
And alle mi sones forth with me
1665 Schal com to thi socour;   *assistance*
For the priis of hethen lond   *victory*
Thou hast thurth douhtines of hond   *bravery in battle*
Wonne with gret vigour."

"Erl Jonas," than seyd Sir Gii,
1670 "Mi leve frende, gramerci.   *dear; many thanks*
For thi gode wille
Than schustow hire me al to dere
To give me thi lond in swiche maner;
Therof nought Y nille.[1]
1675 To your owen cuntré wendeth hom,   *return*
God biteche Y you everichon;   *God be with you all*
Mi way ichil fulfille."   *pilgrimage; complete*
Thai went and kist him everi man,
Th'erl so sore wepe bigan
1680 That might him no man stille.   *No man was able to quieten him*

Th'erl to Durras went anon
And his sones everichon
Were scaped out of care.   *escaped from danger*
Gii than in his way is nome.   *took his way*
1685 For that the geaunt was overcome   *Because*
Ful blithe than was he thare.
Into Grece than went he
And sought halwen of that cuntré   *shrines*
The best that ther ware.
1690 Sethe forth in his way he yede   *Afterwards; went*
Thurthout mani uncouthe thede,   *strange lands*
To Costentyn he is yfare.   *has traveled*

When Gii in Costentin hadde be
Out of that lond than went he
1695 Walkand in the strete   *Walking*
On pilgrimage in his jurnay
His bedes bidand night and day   *prayers reciting*
His sinnes forto bete.   *to atone for*
In Almaine than went he, ywis,   *Germany*
1700 Ther he was sumtime holden of gret pris.   *at one time held in great esteem*
He com to a four way lete   *crossroads*

---

[1] Lines 1672–74: *Then you would pay me far too highly / To give me your lands like this; / I will have none of them*

Biyonde Espire, that riche cité,   *Spires*
Under a croice was maked of tre,   *wooden cross*
A pilgrim he gan mete,

1705 That wrong his honden and wepe sore   *Who wrung; hands*
And curssed the time that he was bore,
"Allas!" it was his song.
"Wayleway," he seyd, "that stounde!   *time*
Wickedliche icham brought to grounde
1710 With wel michel wrong."
Sir Gii went to him tho,
"Man," he seys, "whi farstow so?   *why do you behave like this*
So God geve thee joie to fong,[1]
Tel me what thi name it be
1715 And whi thou makest thus gret pité,
Me thenke thi paynes strong."   *I think you suffer greatly*

"Gode man," seyd the pilgrim tho,
"What hastow to frein me so?   *What [reason] have you to ask*
Swiche sorwe icham in sought   *afflicted*
1720 That thei Y told thee alle mi care,   *though*
For thee might Y never the better fare;   *Through*
To grounde ich am so brought."
"Yis," seyd Gii, "bi the gode Rode,   *holy Cross*
Conseyl Y can give thee gode
1725 And tow telle me thi thought,   *If you*
For oft it falleth uncouthe man   *often; befalls a stranger*
That gode conseyle give can,
Therfore hele it nought."   *conceal*

"For God," he seyd, "thou seyst ful wel.   *By God*
1730 Sumtime ich was, bi Seyn Mighel,   *At one time; Saint Michael*
An erl of gret pousté.   *power*
Thurth al Cristendom, ywis,
Ich was teld a man of gret pris   *spoken of as; wealth*
And of gret bounté;   *prowess*

---

[1] *As surely as God gives you salvation to hope for*

71

1735 And now icham a wroche beggare.   *wretched*
No wonder thei icham ful of care   *though*
Allas, wel wo is me."
For sorwe he might speke namore;   *no more*
He gan to wepe swithe sare   *very bitterly*
1740 That Gii hadde of him pité.

Than seyd the pilgrim, "Thou hast gret wrong
To frain me of mi sorwe strong   *ask; severe*
And might nought bete mi nede.   *remedy*
To begge mi brede Y mot gon,   *must*
1745 Sethen yistay at none ete Y non   *Since yesterday*
Also God me rede."   *As God guides me*
"Yis, felawe," quath Gii, "hele it naught.   *do not keep it secret*
Telle me whi thou art in sorwe braught,
The better thou schalt spede   *get along*
1750 And sethen we schul go seche our mete.   *after that; food*
Ichave a pani of old biyete,   *a penny got long ago*
Thou schalt have half to mede."   *as a gift*

"Gramerci, sir," than seyd he,
"And alle the soth Y schal telle thee.
1755 Erl Tirri is mi name,
Of Gormoys th'erls sone Aubri.   *Worms*
Ich hadde a felawe that hight Gii,   *was called*
A baroun of gode fame.
For the douk of Pavi Sir Otoun   *Pavin*
1760 Hadde don him oft gret tresoun
He slough him with gret grame.   *anger*
Now is his neve th'emperour steward,   *his (Otoun's) nephew the emperor's*
His soster sone that hat Berard;   *sister's son who is called*
He has me don alle this schame.

1765 "Th'emperour he hath served long
For he is wonderliche strong   *extraordinarily*
And of michel might.
He no cometh in non batayle
That he no hath the maistri saunfayl,   *victory without fail*
1770 So egre he is to fight.

In this warld is man non
That ogaines him durst gon,
Herl, baroun, no knight,
And he loked on him with wrake — *hostility*
1775 That his hert no might quake — *shudder with fear*
So stern he is of sight. — *frightening in appearance*

"And for his scherewdhed Sir Berard — *wickedness*
Th'emperour hath made him his steward
To wardi his lond about. — *govern*
1780 Ther nis no douk in al this lond — *duke*
That his hest dar withstonde — *command; deny*
So michel he is dout. — *greatly he is feared*
Yif a man be loved with him — *by*
Be he never so pouer of kin
1785 And he wil to him lout — *bow*
He maketh hem riche anonright, — *him*
Douk, erl, baroun, or knight,
To held with him gret rout. — *stand with him [in a] great retinue*

"And yif a man with him hated be — *be hated by him*
1790 Be he never so riche of fe — *property*
He flemeth him out of lond. — *banishes*
Anon he schal ben todrawe — *dismembered*
Als tite he schal ben yslawe — *As quickly*
And driven him al to schond. — *ruin*
1795 So it bifel our emperour
Held a parlement of gret honour, — *conference*
For his erls he sent his sond. — *summons*
Y come thider with michel prede — *great display*
With an hundred knightes bi mi side
1800 At nede with me to stonde. — *stand*

"And when Y come unto the court
The steward with wicked pourt — *demeanor*
To me he gan to reke. — *run*
He bicleped me of his emes ded — *accused me of his uncle's death*
1805 And seyd he was sleyn thurth mi red; — *decree*
On me he wald be wreke. — *revenged*

73

	And when ich herd that chesoun	*accusation*
	Of the doukes deth Otoun	*Duke Otoun's death*
	Mine hert wald tobreke.	
1810	To th'emperour Y layd mi wedde an heighe	*pledge at once*
	To defende me of that felonie	
	That he to me gan speke.	*Of which he accused me*
	"No wonder thei Y war fordredde;	*though I was frightened*
	Th'emperour tok bothe our wedde	*accepted; pledges*
1815	As Y thee telle may	
	For in alle the court was ther no wight,	*person*
	Douk, erl, baroun, no knight,	
	That durst me borwe that day.	*dared become surety for me*
	Th'emperour comand anon	
1820	Into his prisoun Y schuld be don	
	Withouten more delay.	
	Berard went and sesed mi lond,	*possessed*
	Mine wiif he wald have driven to schond,	*brought to disgrace*
	With sorwe sche fled oway.	
1825	"Than was ich with sorwe and care	
	Among min fomen nomen thare	*enemies taken*
	And don in strong prisoun.	*put in*
	Min frendes token hem to rede,	*sought advice*
	To th'emperour thai bisought and bede	*entreated and begged*
1830	To pay for me ransoun.	
	Th'emperour and Sir Berard	
	Deliverd me bi a forward	*released; agreement*
	And bi this enchesoun:	*condition*
	Y schuld seche mi felawe Gii	*friend*
1835	To defende ous of that felonie	
	Of the doukes deth Otoun.	
	"Out of this lond went Y me	*I took myself*
	And passed over the salt se,	*sea*
	In Inglond Y gan rive;	*came to shore*
1840	At Warwike ichim sought,	
	When Y com thider Y fond him nought	
	Wo was me olive.	*I was ever so wretched*

No Sir Herhaud fond Y nought tare;   *there*
To seche Gyes sone he is fare
1845   That was stollen with strive.   *stolen by force*
Therfore Y wot that Gii is ded,   *believe*
For sorwe can Y me no red —   *I cannot guide myself*
Mine hert wil breke o five."   *into five [pieces]*

Sir Gii biheld Tirri ful right   *directly*
1850   That whilom was so noble a knight   *once*
And lord of michel mounde.   *power*
His bodi was sumtim wele yschredde,   *attired*
Almost naked it was bihedde   *seen*
With sorwe and care ful bounde.   *overcome*
1855   His legges that wer sumtime hosed wel   *furnished with leg-wear*
Tobrosten he seighe hem everidel.   *Blistered; saw; all over*
"Allas," seyd Gii, "that stonde!"
For sorwe that he hadde tho
Word might he speke no mo   *more*
1860   Bot fel aswon to grounde.

Sir Tirri anon com to him than
And in his armes up him nam   *took*
And cleped opon him thare.   *spoke to*
"Man," he said, "what aileth thee?
1865   Thou art ivel at aise so thenketh me,   *disturbed*
Hard it is thi fare."   *Afflicted; behavior*
Sir Gii answerd therafter long,   *after a long pause*
"This ivel greveth me so strong   *misfortune*
In erthe Y wold Y ware,   *the earth (i.e., a grave)*
1870   For sethen that Y was first man
Nas never sorwe on me cam
That greved me so sare."

"Than," seyd Tirri, "felawe, ywis,
Today a yer gon it is
1875   Out of this lond Y went
To seche Gii mi gode frende.
Y no finde nought fer no hende,
Therfore icham al schent.   *ruined*

For now it is teld me our emperer
1880 Hath taken a parlement of this maner
For mi love verrament   *truly*
That douk no erl in his lond be
That he no schal be at that semblé   *assembly*
For to here mi jugement.

1885 "And now no lenge abide Y no may   *delay*
That ne me bihoveth hom this day[1]
Other forto lese min heved.   *Or else; head*
Th'emperour ichave mi treuthe yplight   *sworn my oath*
Y schal bring Sir Gii tonight
1890 To fight ogain that qued   *against; scoundrel*
To fende ous of that felonie   *defend*
Ogain the douke Berard of Pavi
Al of his emes ded.   *uncle's death*
Y wot wele yif Y thider fare
1895 Thai schal me sle with sorwe and care,
Certes Y can no red."   *speak (mention it)*

Gii biheld Tirri with wepeand eighe   *weeping eyes*
And seighe him al that sorwe dreighe   *saw; suffer*
That was him lef and dere.   *beloved*
1900 "Allas," thought Gii, "that ich stounde *Alas; each time*
That Tirri is thus brought to grounde;
So gode felawes we were."   *Such loyal friends*
He thought, "Might Y mete that douke   *were I to*
His heved Y schuld smite fro the bouke *trunk [of the body]*
1905 Or hong him bi the swere.   *neck*
Y no lete for al this warldes won *prevent (stop); wealth*
That Y no schuld the traitour slon
To wreke Tirri mi fere."   *revenge; friend*

"Tirri," seyd Gii, "lat be thi thought.
1910 Ywis, it helpeth thee right nought,   *not at all*
For sorwe it wil thee schende.   *destroy*

---

[1] *That nephew (i.e., Berard) obliges me [to return] home today*

To court go we bothe yfere,   *together*
Gode tidinges we schul ther here   *hear*
Swiche grace God may sende.   *Such*
1915 Have gode hert, dred thee no del   *fear you not one bit*
For God schal help thee ful wel
So curteys He is and hende."
Up risen tho knightes tuo   *those*
With michel care and ful of wo
1920 To courtward thai gan wende

And as thai went tho knightes fre
To courtward in her jurné
Ful bold thai were and yepe.   *eager*
"Allas," Sir Tirri seyd tho,   *then*
1925 "Ich mot rest er ich hennes go
Or mi liif wil fro me lepe."   *pass*
"For God, felawe," than seyd Gii,
"Ly doun and Y schal sitt thee bi   *beside you*
And feir thine heved up kepe."   *support your head*
1930 And when he hadde thus yseyd
On Gyes barm his heved he leyd,   *lap*
Anon Tirri gan slepe.

And when Sir Tirri was fallen on slepe
Sir Gii biheld him and gan to wepe
1935 And gret morning gan make.
Than seighe he an ermine com of his mouthe,   *ermine; from; mouth*
Als swift as winde that bloweth on clouthe   *cloud*
As white as lilii on lake,
To an hille he ran withouten obade,   *delay*
1940 At the hole of the roche in he glade;   *cleft in the rock; slipped*
Gii wonderd for that sake.   *on account of that*
And when he out of that roche cam
Into Tirries mouthe he nam,   *entered*
Anon Tirri gan wake.

1945 Sir Gii was wonderd of that sight   *amazed at*
And Tirri sat up anonright
And biheld Gii opon.   *looked upon*

Than seyd Tirri, "Fader of Heven,
Sir pilgrim, swiche a wonder sweven *amazing dream*
1950 Me met now anon, *I dreamed just now*
That to yon hille that stont on heighe *rises above*
That thou may se with thin eighe
Me thought that Y was gon *dreamed (imagined)*
And at an hole in Y wond *went*
1955 And so riche tresour as Y fond *such*
Y trow in this world is non. *reckon; none [more rich]*

"Biside that tresour lay a dragoun *dragon*
And theron lay a swerd broun, *on top of it; polished*
The sckauberk comly corn. *scabbard beautifully carved*
1960 In the hilt was mani precious ston,
As bright as ani sonne it schon
Withouten oth ysworn. *(i.e., Unquestionably)*
And me thought Gii sat at min heved
And in his lappe me biweved[1]
1965 Astow dest me biforn. *As you did; before (earlier)*
Lord merci, and it wer so *if it were*
Wele were me than bigo *endowed [with wealth]*
That ever yete was Y born."

"Now felawe," seyd Gii, "bi mi leuté *by my honor*
1970 That sweven wil turn gret joie to thee *dream; bring about great happiness to you*
And wele Y schal it rede. *accurately; interpret*
Thurth Gii thou schalt thi lond kever. *recover*
Trust wele to God thei thou be pouer *though; poor*
The better thou schalt spede. *get along [in life]*
1975 To the hulle nim we the way *hill take*
Ther thee thought the tresour lay *dreamed*
And in thou schalt me lede.
Now God that schope al mankinde
Wald we might that tresour finde
1980 It wald help ous at nede." *in our time of need*

---

[1] Lines 1963–64: *And I dreamed that Guy sat at my head / And wrapped me in the loose folds of his shirt*

78

	Up risen tho knightes tuay	*two*
	And to the hille thai nom the way	*took*
	And in thai went ful even	*directly*
	And founde the tresour and the dragoun	
1985	And the swerd of stiel broun	*shining*
	As Tirri mett in his sweven.	*met; dream*
	Sir Gii drough out that swerd anon	
	And alle the pleynes therof it schon	*all of its surfaces shone*
	As it were light of leven.	*a flash of lightning*
1990	"Lord," seyd Gii, "Y thanke Thi sond	*give thanks for Your gift*
	Y seighe never are swiche a brond;	*I never before saw such a sword*
	Y wot it com fram Heven."	*believe*
	Sir Gii gan the hilt bihold	
	That richeliche was graven with gold,	*engraved*
1995	Of charbukel the pomel.	*carbuncle-stone*
	Into the sckaweberk ogain he it dede	*scabbard; put*
	And seyd to Tirri in that stede,	
	"Bi God and Seyn Mighel,	*Saint Michael*
	Of alle this riche tresore	
2000	Y no kepe therof no more	
	Bot this brond of stiel."	*Except; sword*
	[. . .]	
	[. . .]	
	[. . .]	
2005	To courtward tho knightes went	
	To aspie after the parlement;	*look for*
	For drede wald thai nought lete.	*fear; give up*
	Ac Tirri was aferd ful sare	
	Of his fomen be knowen thare	
2010	In the cité yif he sete.[1]	
	Therfore thai toke her ostel gode	*lodging*
	At an hous withouten the toun stode	
	Al bi a dern strete.	*secluded*

---

[1] Lines 2008–10: *But Tirri was terribly afraid / Of being recognized by his enemies / If he entered the city*

Of al night Gii slepe nought,
2015 So michel his hert was ever in thought
With Douk Berard to mete.

Erlich amorwe than ros Gii
And bisought God and our Levedi
He schuld scheld him fro blame   *They; protect; sin*
2020 And seyd to Sir Tirri the hende,
"Kepe me wele this swerd, leve frende,   *Look after for me; dear*
Til Y sende therfore bi name,
And Y schal go to court this day
And yif Y the douke mete may
2025 Y schal gret him with grame;   *anger*
And yif he say ought bot gode,
Bi Him that schadde for ous His blod
Him tit a warld schame."   *Public disgrace will befall him*

Gii goth to toun with michel hete,   *haste*
2030 Th'emperour fram chirche he gan mete
And gret him with anour.   *greeted*
"Lord," seyd Gii, "that with hond   *who*
Made wode, water, and lond,
Save thee, sir emperour.
2035 Icham a man of fer cuntré
And of thi gode, *par charité*,   *"out of kindness"*
Ich axse to mi socour."   *ask; help (provision)*
Th'emperour seyd, "To court come
And of mi gode thou schalt have some   *goods*
2040 For love of Seyn Savour."   *the Holy Savior*

To court thai went al and some,
Th'emperour dede Gii biforn him come,
"Pilgrim," than seyd he,
"Thou art wel weri me thenketh now.
2045 Fram wiche londes comestow?   *do you come*
For thi fader soule telle me."   *father's soul (an oath)*
"Sir," seyd Gii, "ich understond
Ichave ben in mani lond
Biyond the Grekis Se:

80

2050	In Jerusalem and in Surry,	*Syria*
	In Costentin and in Perci	*Persia*
	A gode while have ich be."	
	"Sir pilgrim," seyd th'emperour fre,	
	"What speketh man in that lond of me	
2055	When thou com thennesward?"[1]	
	Sir Gii answerd, "Bi the gode Rode	*Cross*
	Men speketh thee ther ful litel gode	
	Bot tidinges schrewed and hard;	*Only; malicious; harsh*
	For thou hast schent so th'erl Tirri	*ruined*
2060	And other barouns that ben hendy	*noble*
	For love of thi steward.	
	Gret sinne it is to thee	
	To stroye so thi barouns fre	*devastate*
	Al for a fals schreward."	*rogue*
2065	When the douk herd him speke so	
	As a wilde bore he lepe him to	
	His costes for to schawe,	*ribs; carve*
	With his fest he wald have smiten Gii	*fist*
	Bot barouns held him owy,	*back*
2070	Wele tuenti on a rawe.	*twenty all together*
	He seyd to Gii, "Vile traitour,	*evildoer*
	Ner thou bifor th'emperour	*Were you not*
	Thei Y wende to ben tohewe	*Though*
	Bi thi berd Y schuld thee schokke	*shake*
2075	That al thi teth it schuld rokke,	*rock*
	For thou art a kinde schrewe.	*utter rogue*
	"Bi thi semblaunt se men may	*appearance men may see*
	Thou hast ben traitour mani a day —	
	God gif thee schame and schond.	*disgrace and dishonor*
2080	Yif that Y thee mai overgon	*catch*
	To wicked ded thou schalt be don	*a horrible death; put*
	As a traitour to ly in bond,	*Like; shackles*

---

[1] Lines 2054–55: *What do the men of those lands that you have come from say about me?*

81

	In swiche a stede thou schalt be	
	This seven winter no schaltow se	
2085	Noither fet no hond.[1]	
	So schal men chasti foule glotuns	*punish wicked wretches*
	That wil missay gode barouns	*slander*
	That lordinges ben in lond."	*high-ranking lords*

	"Ow sir," seyd Gii, "ertow thas?	
2090	Y nist no nar hou it was[2]	
	Bi the gode Rode.	
	And now Y wot that thou art he,	*know; are he [as has been rumored]*
	Thou art uncurteys so thenketh me.	*ill-behaved*
	Thou farst astow wer wode,	*behave; mad*
2095	And art a man of fair parage	*good ancestry*
	Ycom thou art of heighe linage	
	And of gentil blod.	*noble stock*
	It is thee litel curteysie	*It is no compliment to you*
	To do me swiche vilanie	
2100	Bifor th'emperour ther Y stode.	

	"And for thee wil Y wond no thing,	*hold nothing back*
	Y schal telle thee the sothe withouten lesing	*truth without falsehood*
	Bifor his barouns ichon,	*(i.e., the emperor's)*
	That with gret wrong and sinne, ywis,	*truly*
2105	Th'erl Tirri deshirrite is	*dispossessed (disinherited)*
	And other gode mani on.	*many other persons*
	A thousend men ichave herd teld	*heard say*
	Bothe in toun and in feld	
	As wide as ichave gon	*everywhere I've been*
2110	That he is giltles of that dede	*innocent; crime*
	Thou berst on him with falshede,	*falsely accuse*
	Thin eme he schuld slon."	*uncle; had killed*

	The douk Berrard was wroth,	
	Bi Jhesu Crist he swore his oth.	*oath*

---

[1] Lines 2084–85: *These seven years you will not see / Neither your feet nor hands*

[2] Lines 2089–90: *"Oh! sir," said Guy, "are you thus [such a one]? / I knew no better who it was["]*

2115	"Y wald that thou were Gii	*wish*
	Or that thou so douhti were	
	Thou durst fight for him here	
	God gaf it and our Levedi."	*grant*
	Sir Gii answerd, "Bi Seyn Savour,	
2120	Drede thee nothing, vile traitour,	*Fear not [on that account]*
	Therto icham redy.	*To do that*
	Bi thou wroth, be thou gladde,	*Be you*
	To th'emperour Y gif mi wedde	*make my pledge*
	To fight for th'erl Tirri."	

2125	The douk Berard ther he stode	
	Stared on Gii as he wer wode	
	And egrelich seyd his thought.	
	"Pilgrim," he seyd, "Thou art ful stout,	*bold*
	Ywis, thi wordes that er so prout	*proud*
2130	Schal be ful dere abought.	*dearly paid for*
	Y warn thee wele," he seyd tho,	
	"That thine heved thou schalt forgo	*lose*
	Whereso thou may be sought."	*Wherever you might look*
	Sir Gii seyd, "Than thou it hast	*When*
2135	Than make therof thi bast;	*Then you may brag of it*
	For yete no getes thou it nought."	*you have not got it yet*

	Bifor th'emperour than come Gii	
	And seyd, "Sir Berard of Pavi	
	Is a man of mighti dede,	
2140	And fram fer cuntres comen icham	
	And am a sely pouer man;	*lowly poor*
	Y no have here no sibbered	*relatives*
	No Y no have wepen no armour bright;	*Nor*
	For the love of God Almight	
2145	Finde me armour and stede."	
	Th'emperour answerd, "Bi Jhesu,	
	Pilgrim, thou schalt have anow	*enough*
	Of al that thee is nede."	

	The douk Berrard thennes he went;	
2150	His hert was in strong turment	*great agony*

83

	He no wist what he do might.	*knew not*
	Th'emperour cleped his douhter a mayde,	*daughter*
	"Leve douhter," to hir he seyd,	*Dearest*
	"Kepe this pilgrim tonight."	*Attend to*
2155	Sche him underfenge ful mildeliche	*showed hospitality; graciously*
	And dede bathe him ful softliche,	*tenderly*
	In silke sche wald him dight.	
	Ac therof was nothing his thought;	
	Bot of gode armour he hir bisought[1]	
2160	With the douke Berard to fight.	

	Amorwe aros that emperour	*In the morning*
	Erls, barouns of gret honour,	
	To chirche with him thai yede.	*went*
	And when the barouns asembled was	
2165	Than might men sen in that plas	*see*
	Togider a fair ferred.	*fine company*
	Thider com the douk Berard,	
	Prout and stern as a lipard,	*leopard*
	Wele yarmed on stede	*Properly armed on horseback*
2170	And priked right as he wer wode	*spurred [on his horse]*
	Among the barouns ther thai stode	
	Batayle forto bede.	*to offer*

	The maiden forgat never a del	*not one thing*
	The pilgrim was armed ful wel	
2175	With a gode glaive in honde	*spear*
	And a swift-ernand stede;	*swift-galloping*
	Al wrin sche dede him lede	*Fully equipped; bring*
	The best of that lond.	
	Than Sir Gii him bithought	*remembered*
2180	The gode swerd forgat he nought	
	That he in tresour fond.	*treasure found*
	He sent therafter priveliche —	*for it secretly*

---

[1] Lines 2157–59: *She wanted to dress him in silk. / But this was not his desire; / The only thing he asked her for was good armor*

No man wist litel no miche —   *knew anything [about it]*
And Tirri sent him the brond.

2185 When that mayden hadde graithed Gii   *dressed*
       Wele ydight and ful richely   *equipped*
       Men gan on him biheld.
       Sche ledde him forth swithe stille,   *very meekly*
       To th'emperour with gode wille
2190 Sche taught him forto weld.   *delivered him; fight*
       Than seyd th'emperour hende and fre,
       "Lordinges, listen now to me
       Bothe yong and eld:
       This knight that ye se now here
2195 Hath taken batail in strong maner   *undertaken; bravely*
       Al forto fight in feld.   *field*

       "This knight," he seyd, "that stount me bi
       Wil fight for th'erl Sir Tirri —
       For nothing wil he wond —   *On no account; shrink back [for fear]*
2200 And defende him of that felonie   *(i.e., Tirri)*
       Ogain the douk Berard of Pavi   *Against*
       That he berth him an hond;   *accuses; assuredly*
       For Tirri is out of lond went
       To seche Gii verrament
2205 That for him might stond.   *represent in battle*
       This day is sett bituen hem tuo
       Or be deshirrite forevermo   *deprived [of land and possessions]*
       And flemed out of lond.   *outlawed*

       "Bot now is comen here this knight,
2210 Ogain Berard hath taken the fight
       For nothing wil he flen.   *flee*
       Ac, lordinges," he seyd, "everichon   *But; each of you*
       Where the batayl schal be don
       Loke where it may best ben."   *Consider*
2215 Than loked thai it schuld be   *determined*
       In a launde under the cité.   *plain*
       Thider in thai went biden.   *immediately*
       Mani man bad God that day   *prayed*

	Help the pilgrim as He wele may	
2220	The douk Berard to slen.	*slay*
	On hors lopen tho knightes prest	*leaped those; at once*
	And lopen togider til schaftes brest	*attacked each other; broke*
	That strong weren and trewe;	*sturdy; reliable*
	And her gerthes brusten that strong were	*their saddle girths burst apart*
2225	And tho knightes bothe yfere	*simultaneously*
	Out of her sadels threwe.	*were thrown*
	After thai drough her swerdes gode	*drew*
	And leyd on as thai were wode	*rained down blows; mad (i.e., frenziedly)*
	That were gode and newe.	*(i.e., their swords)*
2230	And astow sest the fir on flint,	
	The stem out of her helmes stint	
	So hetelich thai gun hewe. [1]	
	Wele wer armed tho knightes stout	
	Bot he had more yren him about,	*iron*
2235	That fals Berardine.	
	Tuay hauberkes he was in weved	*Two coats of mail; wrapped in*
	And tuay helmes opon his heved	
	Was wrought in Sarayine.	*Saracen lands*
	Opon his schulder henge a duble scheld	*double shield*
2240	Beter might non be born in feld,	
	A gode swerd of stiel fine.	
	Mani man therwith his liif had lorn;	
	It was sumtim therbiforn	
	The kinges Costentine.	
2245	Strong batayl held tho knightes bold	
	That alle that ever gan hem bihold	*[So] that*
	Thai seyden hem among	*said to one another*
	The pilgrim was non erthely man;	
	It was an angel from Heven cam	
2250	For Tirri batayle to fong.	*undertake*

---

[1] Lines 2230–32: *In the same way that one sees sparks come from flint, / Steam rose from their helmets / Since they struck so violently*

For mani gode erl and mani baroun
Berard hath ybrought adoun
With wel michel wrong.
Therfore hath God sent, ywis,
2255   An angel out of heven-blis
To sle that traitour strong.

Al the folk in that cité was,   *who lived*
Litel and michel, more and las,   *Small and large, rich and poor*
To se the batayl thai yede.   *went*
2260   Bot Tirri in a chirche liis   *hides*
And ever he bisought God, ywis,   *entreated; truly*
He schuld him help and spede.   *assist*
When he herd telle that the pilgrim
Faught ogain the douke Berardin
2265   To help him at his nede.
Wel fain he wald thider gon   *Very eagerly; wished to go*
Bot for knoweing of his fon
Wel sore he gan him drede.[1]

Ac natheles he ros up tho
2270   With michel care and michel wo   *great suffering; distress*
And thider he went wel swithe.   *very quickly*
When he com to the plas
Ther the bataile loked was   *decreed*
Amonges hem he gan lithe   *the people; walk*
2275   And when he seyghe the douk so strong   *saw*
And his armes tohewe among,   *smashed repeatedly*
In his hert he was ful blithe.   *joyful*
And tho he seyghe his blod spille,   *when*
God he thonked with gode wille
2280   [. . .]

---

[1] Lines 2267–68: *But at [the thought of] being recognized by his enemies / He became extremely fearful*

"Lord, merci," Tirri gan say,
"This is nought the pilgrim Y met yisterday
That is so richeliche dight.
He was a feble pouer body   *individual*
2285   Sely, messays, and hungri,   *Humble, impoverished; starved*
And he is of michel might.
Y trow non erthelich man it be,   *earthly (of this world)*
On Gii Y thenke when ichim se
So douhti he was in fight.   *strong; in battle*
2290   Yif Gii mi felawe now ded nere   *were not dead*
Ich wald sigge that he it were   *say*
So liche thai ben of sight."   *So alike they appear*

Into chirche ogain he yede   *once again; went*
And fel on knes in that stede
2295   And Jhesus Crist he bisought
He schuld help the pilgrim
That faught ogain Douk Berardin
That miche wo hath him wrought.
Hard togider gun thai fight
2300   Fro the morwe to the night   *morning*
That thai rest hem nought.
And when hem failed light of day
Thai couthe no rede what thai do may.[1]
To th'emperour thai hem brought.   *they led them*

2305   "Sir emperour," thai seyd anon,
"What schul we with this knightes don?   *these; do*
At thi wille schal it be."
Th'emperour clept to him tho   *called*
Four barouns that his trust was to.   *that he had confidence in*
2310   "Lordinges," than seyd he,
"Kepe me wele the Douk Berard,   *Guard for me*
And bring him tomorwe bi a forward,   *agreement*
Open al your fe;   *Upon forfeit of your wealth*
And Y schal kepe the pilgrim tonight;

---

[1] Lines 2302–03: *When the light of day failed them / They could not decide what they should do*

2315	Til tomorwe that it is day light	*when*
	He schal bileve with me."	*remain*
	Than departed this batayle,	
	Tho four barouns withouten fayl	
	Understode Berard to kepe	*Accepted [under their charge]*
2320	And th'emperour toke the pilgrim	
	In a chaumber to loken him	*lock*
	With serjaunce wise and yepe.	*guards able; clever*
	The douke Berard forgat him nought;	
	Of a foule tresoun he him bithought:[1]	
2325	Four knightes he gan clepe.	*summoned*
	"For mi love," he seyd, "goth tonight	*go*
	Ther the pilgrim lith ful right	*Directly to where the pilgrim lies*
	And sleth him in his slepe."	*kill*
	Thai armed hem swithe wel	*themselves very*
2330	Bothe in iren and in stiel	
	And went hem forth in hast,	
	Into the chaumber thai went anon.	
	The pilgrims kepers everichon	
	Lay and slepe ful fast.	*Lay asleep; soundly*
2335	To the pilgrim thai went ful right	
	And left up the bedde with her might	*lifted*
	Tho four traitours unwrast.	*wicked*
	To the se thai beren him	*sea; carried*
	And bothe bed and the pilgrim	
2340	Into the see thai cast.	*threw*
	To Sir Berard thai went anon	
	And teld him hou thai hadden don,	
	Therof he was ful fawe.	*pleased*
	"Sir," thai seyd, "be nought adred.	*do not worry*
2345	Bothe the pilgrim and the bed	
	Into the se we han ythrawe."	*have thrown*
	The pilgrim waked and loked an heyghe,	*looked up*

---

[1] Lines 2323–24 *Duke Berard did not forget about him (Guy); / He devised a wicked plan*

89

	The sterres on the heven he seighe,	*stars*
	The water about him drawe.	*washed*
2350	Thei he was ferd no wonder it nis;	*If he was afraid it is no surprise*
	Non other thing he no seyghe, ywis,	
	Bot winde and wateres wawe.	*Only wind and water's wave*

"Lord," seyd Gii, "God Almight
That winde and water and al thing dight   *made*
2355   On me have now pité.
Whi is me fallen thus strong cumbring?[1]
And Y no fight forto win nothing —   *I don't fight to win anything*
Noither gold no fe,
For no cité no no castel —   *nor*
2360   Bot for mi felawe Y loved so wel   *friend*
That was of gret bounté,   *goodness*
For he was sumtyim so douhti   *Because; once so excellent*
And now he is so pouer a bodi.   *unfortunate an individual*
Certes it reweth me."   *Truly; pains*

2365   Now herkeneth a litel striif   *hear; narrative*
Hou He saved the pilgrims liif,
Jhesu that sitt in trone,   *throne*
With a fischer that was comand   *fisherman; approaching (coming)*
In the se fische takeand   *sea; taking*
2370   Bi himself alon.
He seth that bed floter him by   *sees; float*
"On Godes half!" he gan to cri,   *On God's behalf!*
"What artow? Say me son."   *Who are you? Tell me immediately*
The pilgrim his heved upplight   *raised up*
2375   And crid to him anonright
And made wel reweli mon.   *pitiful cry*

"Gode man," than seyd he,
"Y leve on God in Trinité   *believe in*
The sothe thou schalt now sen.
2380   Understode thou ought of the batayl hard   *Know; anything; fierce*

---

[1] *Why have I been cast into this terrible misfortune*

Bituen the pilgrim and Sir Berard
Hou thai foughten bituen?"   *together*
The fischer seyd, "Y seighe the fight   *saw*
Fro the morwe to the night,
2385 For nothing wald thai flen.   *retreat*
Th'emperour comand tho   *commanded*
Thai schuld be kept bothe tuo   *guarded both of them*
Tomorwe bring hem oghen."

"Icham," he seyd, "the pilgrim
2390 That faught with the douke Berardin
For Tirri the hendi knight.
Yistreven we wer deled ato,   *Yesterday evening; separated*
In a chaumber Y was do   *put away*
With serjaunce wise and wight.   *guards; strong*
2395 Hou Ich com her no wot Y nought;   *here*
For His love that this warld hath wrought
Save me yif thou might."   *if you can*
The fischer tok him into his bot anon
And to his hous he ladde him hom   *home*
2400 And saved his liif that night.

Th'emperour ros amorwe, ywis,
And at the chirche he herd his messe   *mass*
In the first tide of the day   *service*
And into his halle he gan gon
2405 And after the steward he axed anon   *asked*
And the pilgrim withouten delay.
The four barouns forgat hem nought,   *had done their duty*
The douke Berard thai han forth brought
Redy armed to play.   *fight*
2410 And the pilgrims kepers com everichon
And seyd to th'emperour, bi Seyn Jon,
The pilgrim was oway.   *gone from the place*

Th'emperour was wel wroth,
Bi his fader soule he swore his oth
2415 Thai schuld ben hang and drawe.   *hung; drawn*
"For Godes love," he seyd, "Merci,

91

This douke Berard of Pavi
Hath him brought o dawe."   *put him to death*
Th'emperour seyd, "Bi Seyn Martin,
2420   Hastow don this, fals Berardin,
To don the pilgrim slawe?   *cause the pilgrim to be killed*
Yeld him dethes or lives to me   *dead or living*
Or in mi court dempt thou schalt be   *condemned*
Thurth jugement of lawe."

2425   The douke Berard wex wroth and wo,   *grew angry; distressed*
Th'emperour he answerd tho
With wel michel hete,   *intense hatred*
"Ichave served thee long, Sir Emperour,
And kept thi londes with michel anour   *protected; great honor*
2430   And now thou ginnest me threte.   *threaten me*
Therof give Y nought a chirston.   *cherry stone*
Hom to Lombardy ichil gon
With alle the ost Y may gete.   *army*
Y schal com into Almayn for al thi tene   *harm*
2435   Of al thi lond siker mot thou ben   *you may be certain*
O fot Y no schal thee lete."   *One; leave you*

When th'emperour herd that
And of his thretening undergat   *comprehended*
He bad with wordes bold   *demanded*
2440   Out of his court he schuld gon
And he answerd sone anon
That sikerliche he nold.   *certainly; would not*
Ther com the fischer priveliche   *Into that place; discreetly*
And puked th'emperour softliche,   *nudged (poked); gently*
2445   His tale to him he told.
"Sir emperour," he seyd, "listen to me.
Of the pilgrim ichil telle thee
Yif thou me herken wold."

"Fischer," seyd th'emperour fre,   *noble*
2450   "Of the pilgrim telle thou me
Yif thou the sothe can sayn."
"For sothe," he seyd, "Y can ful wel

Y schal thee leyghen never a del; *will not lie to you about the smallest detail*
Therof icham ful fain. *willing*
2455 Yistreven withouten lesing *Yesterday evening*
Y went to the se of fischeing *fishing*
Mine nettes forto layn. *to put out*
A bedde Y fond ther floterand *floating*
And theron a knight liggeand, *lying*
2460 A man of michel mayn. *strength*

"And ich him axed what he were.
He told me the sothe there
With wordes fre and hende.
'Icham,' he seyd, 'the pilgrim
2465 That faught with the douke Berardin
Yisterday to the nende.' *ninth [hour]*
Y tok him into mi bot anon
And to min hous Y lad him hom *led*
And kept him as mi frende. *looked after him like one of my own*
2470 Yif thou levest nought he is thare *do not believe*
Do sum serjaunt thider fare *send*
And ther ye may him fende." *find*

Th'emperour sent after him tho
With the fischer and other mo *other persons beside*
2475 And brought him saunfayle. *without fail*
Thai were don togider blive *(i.e., Guy and Berard); immediately*
With hard strokes forto drive *to strike*
Thai gun hem to asayle.
Wel hard togider gun thai fight,
2480 With her brondes that wer bright
Thai hewe hauberk of mayle.
Thus togider gun thai play *fight*
Til it was the heyghe midday *high noon*
With wel strong batayle.

2485 The douk Berard was egre of mode, *angry*
He smot to Gii as he wer wode *deranged*
His liif he wende to winne. *hoped; take*
He hit him on the helm on hight

93

	That alle the floures feir and bright	*[So] that; ornaments*
2490	He dede hem fleyghe atuinne.	*scatter*
	The nasel he carf atuo	*nose-guard; carved in two*
	And the venteyle he dede also	*face-guard*
	Right to his bare chinne.	
	[. . .]	
2495	[. . .]	
	[. . .]	

	Sir Gii was wroth anon fot-hot	*at once*
	And Berard on the helme he smot;	
	To stond hadde he no space	*stand [against it];chance*
2500	For bothe helmes he carf atuo	
	And his heved he dede also	*head*
	In midward of the face.	*the middle*
	Thurth al his bodi the swerd bot	*cut*
	Into the erthe wele half a fot,	
2505	That seighe men in the place.	
	Th[e s]oule went fro the bodi there,	
	Th[e fol]k of the cite wel glad were,	
	Th[ai] thonked our Lordes grace.	

	Bifor th'emperour than com Sir Gii,	
2510	"Ichave wroken th'erl Tirri —	*avenged*
	The sothe thou might now sen —	
	And defended him of that felonie	
	Ogain the douke Berard of Pavi	
	That was so stout and ken.	*bold and brave*
2515	Therfore the sothe ich ax thee	
	Yif Tirri schal quite-cleymed be	
	And have his lond ogen;	
	And whoso ther ogain withstond	*offers resistance to this*
	He schal have schame of min hond	*be reproached*
2520	Wel siker may he ben."	*certain [of that]*

	Th'emperour seyd, "Sikerly	
	Thou hast wroken th'erl Tirri;	*avenged*
	Gret honour thou hast him don.	
	Therfore when he is come	

2525	His londes than al and some	
	He schal have everichon."	
	Than was Gii glad and blithe	
	And kest of his armes also swithe,	*threw off his armor at once*
	After him he thought to gon.	*him (Tirri); decided*
2530	Th'emperour wald clothe him in gold	*wished to*
	Ac sikerliche he seyd he nold,	*did not desire it*
	His sclavain he axed anon.	*pilgrim's cloak*
	To toun he went in his way	*town; on his journey*
	To finde Tirri yif he may	
2535	In sorwe and care ful bounde.	*overcome*
	Into a chirche he him dede	*went*
	And fond him in a privé stede	*secret (secluded) place*
	Liand on knes to grounde.	*Kneeling*
	"Arise up, Tirri," he seyd tho,	
2540	"To court thou schalt with me go	
	Now ichave thee founde."	
	Tirri anon his heved upbreyd	*lifted up*
	And seyd, "Pilgrim hastow me treyd?	*betrayed me*
	Allas, that ich stounde!	*Alas then!*
2545	"Allas, allas!" than seyd he,	
	"To what man may men trust be	*What man can anyone be confident in*
	To chese to his make?	*To choose as his companion*
	Thou that semed so stedefast	
	To th'emperour me wraied hast,	*betrayed*
2550	To sle me thou hast take.	*kill; decided*
	In ivel time was it to me	*an unlucky time*
	That Y mi name told to thee;	
	Allas that ich sake."	*gave up [my disguise]*
	For sorwe that he hadde tho	
2555	O word no might he speke mo	
	Bot stode and gan to quake.	*tremble*
	"Tirri," seyd Gii, "drede thee nothing,	*do not fear*
	Thou schalt today here gode tiding	*hear*
	Thurth grace of Godes sond.	*God's ordinance*
2560	The schrewed Douke Berard he is ded,	*evil*

95

Under the cité he is yleyde,   *buried*
Y slough him with min hond."
Tho was Tirri glad and blithe,
To court he went also swithe   *at once*
2565 For nothing wald he wond.   *hold back*
"Sir emperour," seyd Gii anon,
"Now is Tirri comen hom
To resceive his lond."

Th'emperour on him gan bihold   *gaze*
2570 And seyd to him with wordes bold,
"Artow th'erl Tirri?   *Are you*
Where is now thi bold chere   *expression*
That whilom so douhti were   *once; brave*
And holden so hardi?"   *considered; courageous*
2575 "Ya, sir," he seyd, "icham he.
Whilom Y was of gret boundé   *prowess*
And helden ful douhti
And now ich have al forlorn
With miche sorwe on even and morn
2580 To seke mi felawe Sir Gii.

"Ich have him sought in mani lond   *sought*
Ac never man yete ich fond
Can telle of him no sawe.   *story*
He is dede ich wot ful wel,   *know*
2585 God Almighti and Seyn Mighel
To blis his soule drawe.   *carry up*
Ac now is it told me this pilgrim
As slayn the douke Berardin;   *Has*
Therof icham ful fawe.   *joyful*
2590 Sir Emperour, Y bid merci,
For Godes love and our Levedi,
Thou do me londes lawe."   *You authorize my lands [as mine] by law*

Thritti erls wel curteys
And alle the lordinges of the paylais
2595 And mani baroun afine   *altogether*
Crid merci to th'emperour bold.

Th'emperour gan him bihold
And seyd, "Tirri, frende min,
Here Y sese thee in al thi lond   *grant legal possession to you*
2600 With worthschip to held in thine hond   *honor; possess*
Bi God and Seyn Martine.
Bifor mi barouns Y graunt thee   *In front of (i.e., witnessed by)*
Steward of mi lond thou schalt be
As was the douke Berardine."

2605 Th'emperour kist him ful swete,   *kissed; amiably*
Forgaf him his wrethe and his hete   *Forgave; anger; hatred*
Bifor hem al there.
When th'emperour and th'erl were at on   *at one (reconciled)*
The lordinges everichon
2610 Wele blithe of hertes were.
"Sir Tirri," seyd th'emperour fre,
"For thi fader soule tel thou me
Astow art me leve and dere,   *to me dear and precious*
Whennes is this pilgrim?   *From where*
2615 Is he thin em or thi cosyin   *uncle*
That faught for thee here?"

"Sir Emperour," seyd Sir Tirri,
"So God me help and our Levedi
For sothe withouten fayle
2620 Y no seighe never ere this pilgrim   *saw; before*
Bot this other day Y met with him   *Apart from; [when] I*
And told him mi conseyl.
He swore as tite bi Seyn Jon   *immediately*
To thi court he wald gon
2625 The douk Berard to asayle.
Ich wend wel litel than, Y plight,   *Little did I know then, I swear*
He hadde ben of michel might
To hold with him batayle."

Th'emperour dede as a gode man
2630 And Tirri into his chaumber he nam   *took*
And richeliche gan him schrede.   *dress*
He fond him wepen and armour bright

97

	And al that schuld falle to knight	*befit*
	And feffed him with prede	*furnished; splendidly*
2635	And fond him hors and stedes gode	
	Of al his lond the best stode	*stock*
	Hom with him to lede.	
	Th'emperour wald the pilgrim athold	*retain*
	Ac sikerliche he seyd he nold,	*But truly; would not*
2640	With Tirri hom he yede.	*went*
	When Tirri was comen hom	
	The pilgrim he wald anon	
	Sesen in al his lond.[1]	
	And he forsoke it al outright	*completely refused it*
2645	For riches loved he no wight	*not one bit*
	For to hold in hond.	*possess*
	Th'erl as swithe his sond he sent	*quickly; command*
	Over al his lond verrament	
	Til that his wiif he fond.	*found*
2650	Tho was sche founden in an ile	*island*
	In a nunri that while	*nunnery during all that time*
	For doute of Berardes bond.	*fear; rule*
	Tho was Tirri a noble man	
	In al that lond better nas nan	*was none*
2655	As Y you tel may.	
	Destrud were al his enemis,	
	He liveth in michel joie and blis	
	Also a prince in play.	*Like; disport*
	Anon Sir Gii him bithought	*decided*
2660	That lenger wald he duelle nought;	
	To Sir Tirri on a day	
	He seyd to him in that tide,	
	"Here nil Y no lenger abide,	*I will*
	Ich mot wende in mi way.	*must continue my journey*

---

[1] Lines 2642–43: *To the pilgrim he immediately wished / To sign over all his land*

98

2665	"O thing," he seyd, "Y pray thee,	*One*
	Out of the cité go with me	
	Astow art hendi knight.	
	Alon we shul go bothe yfere	*Alone; together*
	And swich tidinges thou schalt here	*such*
2670	Thou schalt have wonder, aplight."	*be amazed; in faith*
	Th'erl him graunt with hert fre	*willingly*
	And went with him out of that cité	
	In his way ful right.	
	And when thai wer thennes half a mile	
2675	Ther thai duelled a litel while	*remained*
	Tho gomes of michel might.	*Those men*

	"Tirri," seyd Gii, "understond thou the,	*this*
	Thou art unkinde so thenketh me	*disloyal*
	For Gii thi gode fere;	*Towards; friend*
2680	Whi wiltow him knowe nought?	*recognize*
	Ywis, thou art ivel bithought,	*ill informed*
	No was he thee leve and dere?	*Was he not dear to you*
	Thenke he slough the douk Otoun	*Remember*
	And brought thee out of his prisoun	
2685	And made thee quite and skere	*acquitted (blameless); free*
	And hou he fond thee ded almast	*almost dead*
	As he rode thurth a forest	
	With a rewely chere.	*pitiful expression*

	"And hou he socourd thi leman schene	*rescued; beautiful lady*
2690	And al the fiften outlawes ken	
	He slough hem al on rawe	*all of them*
	And slough the four knightes radde	*quickly*
	And thi bodi to toun ladde	*carried*
	To leche thi woundes ful fawe;	*treat (heal); gladly*
2695	And he socourd thi fader in wer	*assisted; father; battle*
	And halp thee bothe nere and fer	*in every way*
	Tho thou was fallen ful lawe.	*When; low*
	And now Y slough Berard the strong.	
	Icham Gii, thou hast wrong.	*acted unjustly*
2700	Why niltow me nought knawe?"	*will you*

99

When th'erl herd him speke so
Wepen he gan with eyghen to   *to weep; [his] eyes two*
And fel aswon to grounde.
"For Godes love," he seyd, "merci.
2705   Ivel at ese now am Y   *Ill*
In sorwe and care ful bounde.   *completely overcome*
Ful wele might Y knowe thee ar now,   *before*
In al this warld was man bot thou   *was [no] man*
Ogain Berard durst founde.   *[Who would] dare fight against Berard*
2710   Merci, sir, *par charité*;   *Forgive me*
That ich have misknowen thee   *failed to recognize*
Allas, allas, that stounde!   *time*

"Merci!" he crid on his kne,
Bothe for sorwe and for pité
2715   Wepen he bigan.
He seyghe his legges brosten ich del   *blistered all over*
That whilom wer yhosed ful wel   *once; clad*
More sorwe made never man.
Sir Gii went to him tho —   *then*
2720   In his hert him was wo —
And in his armes up him nam.   *took*
Atuix hem was gret diol in that stounde,   *Between; sorrow; time*
Bothe thai fel aswon to grounde
For sorwe thai wex al wan.   *grew; pale*

2725   "Tirri," seyd Sir Gii tho,
"Thou schalt bileve and Y schal go;   *stay*
Y biteche thee heven-king   *I commend you to God*
Bot Ich have a sone, ywis —   *However*
Y not whether he knight is   *know not*
2730   For he is bot a yongling —   *youngster*
Yif he have ani nede to thee   *has any need to [call on] you*
Help him for the love of me
Y pray thee in al thing.   *above all else*
Ich hope he schal be a gode knight,
2735   Y pray Jhesu ful of might
He graunt him His blisceing."   *blessing*

"Merci, sir," than seyd he,
"For Godes love leve her stil with me   *stay here*
Y pray thee *par amour*;   *if you please (of your kindness)*
2740   Mi treuthe Y plight in thine hond   *My loyalty I pledge with a handshake*
Y schal thee sese in al mi lond   *endow*
Bothe in toun and tour.
Thi man Y wil be and serve thee ay   *vassal; always*
Ther while mi liif lest may   *lasts*
2745   To hold up thin honour.
And yif thou no wilt, ichil with thee go;   *will not*
Ywis, ichave wele lever so   *much rather [do] so*
Than bileve with th'emperour."   *remain*

"Do oway, Sir Tirri, therof speke nought,   *Stop this*
2750   Al idel speche it is thi thought.   *foolish*
Wende ogain hom now right   *Return; directly*
And be nought to prout Y thee rede   *too proud; advise*
To serve thi lord at al his nede
Thou prove with thi might.   *demonstrate*
2755   Desirite no man of his lond;   *Deprive*
Yif thou dost thou gos to schond   *disgrace*
Ful siker be thou, aplight.
For yive thou reve a man his fe   *if; rob; [of] his land*
Godes face schaltow never se   *shall you*
2760   No com in heven-light.   *Nor; into [the] light of Heaven*

"Bithenke thee wele of Douke Berard
Hou prout he was for he was steward   *because*
And flemed thee out of lond   *banished*
And he now desirite is,   *disinherited*
2765   With michel sorwe slayn, ywis,
And schamelich driven to schond.   *shamefully; disgrace*
Y schal gon and thou bileve schalt,   *stay*
Y biteche thee God that al thing walt   *entrust you [to]; rules*
And maked with His hond."   *created*
2770   Thai kisten hem togider tho;
Olive thai seyghen hem never eft mo   *saw each other*
As the gest doth ous understond.   *tale tells us (causes us to know)*

Gret sorwe thai made at her parting
And kist hem with eighe wepeing;   *kissed each other; eyes*
2775 Thai wenten hem bothe atuo.   *separate ways*
Als swithe th'erl Tirri went him hom;   *At once*
Thre days he no ete mete non,   *ate nothing*
In hert him was ful wo.
And when the countas sikerly   *countess*
2780 Herd seyn it was Sir Gii
That than was went hem fro
Sche upbreyd hir lord day and night   *reproached*
That he no had holden him with strengthe and might   *restrained him*
And laten him nought thennes gon.   *not let him go away*

2785 Now went Gii forth in his way
Toward the see so swithe he may,   *as quickly [as]*
For Tirri he siked sare.   *sighed*
Into schip he went bilive,   *ship; at once*
Over the se he gan drive,
2790 Into Inglond he gan fare.   *came*
The lond folk he axed anon   *people of that country*
After King Athelston
In what cuntré he ware.   *place*
"At Winchester verrament
2795 And after his barouns he hath sent,
Bothe lasse and mare.

"Erls, barouns, and bischopes,
Knightes, priours, and abbotes
At Winchester thai ben ichon
2800 And han purvayd withouten lesing   *arranged*
Thre days to ben in fasting
To biseke God in tron   *pray to; in majesty*
He sende hem thurth His swet sond   *ordinance*
A man that were douhti of hond   *of great fighting ability*
2805 Ogain Colbrond to gon.   *fight*
Ther is the king and the barnage, ywis,   *nobility*
For doute of her enemis   *fear*
That wayt hem forto slon.

"For Sir Anlaf the king of Danmark
2810   With a nost store and stark   *an army (host) powerful; strong*
       Into Inglond is come
       With fiften thousend knightes of pris,   *excellent*
       Alle this lond thai stroyen, ywis,   *ravage*
       And mani a toun han nome.   *have taken*
2815   A geaunt he hath brought with him   *giant*
       Out of Aufrike stout and grim,   *Africa*
       Colbrond hat that gome.   *was called; creature*
       For him is al Inglond forlore   *Because of him; lost*
       Bot Godes help be bifore   *Unless; is forthcoming*
2820   That socour sende hem some.

       "To the king he hath sent his sond[1]
       Forto yeld him al Inglond   *To surrender [to] him*
       And gif him trowage outright   *tribute*
       Yif he no wil nought finde a baroun,
2825   A geaunt other a champioun,   *or*
       Ogain Colbrond to fight,   *Against*
       And therof thai han taken a day.   *for that; set*
       Ac our king non finde may   *But*
       Erl, baroun, no knight,
2830   No squier, no serjaunt non
       Ogain the geaunt dar gon   *dare fight*
       So grim he is of sight."

       Than seyd Sir Gii, "Whare is Herhaud?
       That in his time was so bald?"
2835   And thai answerd ful swithe.
       "To seche Gyes sone he is fare
       That marchaunce hadde stollen thare,   *merchants; stolen*
       For him he was unblithe."   *sorry*
       "And where is th'erl Rohaut of pris?"   *renown*
2840   And thai answerd, "Dede he is —
       A gode while is go sithe —   *Some time ago*
       And Feliis his douhter is his air,   *heir*

---

[1] *To the king (Athelston) he (Anlaf) has sent his message*

103

So gode a levedi no so fair,   *lady nor*
Ywis, nis non olive."

2845   Gii went to Winchester a ful gode pas   *at great speed*
        Ther the king that time was
        To held his parlement;
        The barouns weren in the halle.
        The king seyd, "Lordinges alle,
2850   Mine men ye ben verrament,
        Therfore ich ax withouten fayl
        Of this Danis folk wil ous aseyl   *Danish*
        Ich biseche you with gode entent,   *in good faith*
        For Godes love Y pray you
2855   Gode conseyl give me now
        Or elles we ben al schent.   *ruined*

        "For the king of Danmark with wrong   *wickedness*
        With his geaunt that is so strong
        He wil ous al schende.   *overcome*
2860   Therfore ich axi you ichon   *each one*
        What rede is best forto don   *counsel*
        Ogaines hem forto wende?
        Yif he overcom ous in batayle
        He wil slen ous alle saunfeyle   *without doubt*
2865   And strouen al our kende.   *destroy; people*
        Than schal Inglond evermo
        Live in thraldom and in wo   *servitude*
        Unto the warldes ende.

        "Therfore ich axi you now right   *directly*
2870   Yif ye knowe our ani knight   *of ours*
        That is so stout and bold
        That the batayle dar take an hond
        To fight ogain Colbrond.
        Half mi lond have he schold
2875   With alle the borwes that lith therto,   *towns; belong to it*
        To him and to his aires evermo
        To have yive he wold."   *if*
        Stil seten erls and barouns   *Silent sat*

104

	As men hadde schaven her crounes;[1]	
2880	Nought on answere nold.	*one*

	"Allas," seyd the king, "that Y was born.	
	Al mi joie it is forlorn,	*utterly lost*
	Wel wo is me olive.	
	Now in al mi lond nis no knight	
2885	Ogains a geant to hold fight	
	Mine hert wil breken on five.	
	Allas of Warwike Sir Gii	
	Y no hadde geven thee half mi lond frely	*If only I had*
	To hold withouten strive;	*dispute*
2890	Wele were me than bifalle.	*Then would I do well*
	Ac certes now the Danis men alle	*surely*
	To sorwe thai schul me drive."	

	When it was night to bedde thai yede;	*went*
	The king for sorwe and for drede	
2895	With teres wett his lere.	*face (cheek)*
	Of al that night he slepe right nought	*not at all*
	Bot ever Jhesu he bisought	
	That was him leve and dere	*[to] him beloved*
	He schuld him sende thurth His sond	*grace*
2900	A man to fight with Colbrond	
	Yif it Is wille were.	*His*
	And Jhesus Crist ful of might	
	He sent him a noble knight	
	As ye may forward here.	*hereafter hear*

	Ther com an angel fram heven-light	
2905	And seyd to the king ful right	
	Thurth grace of Godes sond.	*ordinance*
	He seyd, "King Athelston, slepestow?	*[do] you sleep?*
	Hider me sent thee King Jhesu	*Here I am sent to you by*
2910	To comfort thee to fond.	*To try to*
	Tomorwe go to the north gate ful swithe,	*right away*

---

[1] Lines 2878–79: *Silent sat earls and barons / As men who had shaved their heads (i.e., As monks)*

A pilgrim thou schalt se com bilive   *before long*
When thou hast a while stond.
Bid him for Seynt Charité
2915 That he take the batayl for thee
And he it wil nim on hond."   *take in hand (i.e., undertake)*

Than was the king glad and blithe,
Amorwe he ros up ful swithe
And went to the gate ful right.   *directly*
2920 Tuay erls went with him tho   *Two*
And tuay bischopes dede also.   *did*
The weder was fair and bright.   *weather*
Opon the day about prime
The king seighe cum the pilgrim
2925 Bi the sclavayn he him plight.   *pilgrim's cloak; seized*
"Pilgrim," he seyd, "Y pray thee   *entreat*
To court wende thou hom with me
And ostel ther al night."   *receive lodging*

"Be stille, sir," seyd the pilgrim,
2930 "It is nought yete time to take min in,   *procure lodgings*
Also God me rede."   *As God directs me*
The king him bisought tho   *begged then*
And the lordinges dede also,
To court with hem he yede.
2935 "Pilgrim," quath the king, "*par charité,*
Yif it be thi wil understond to me,
Y schal schewe thee al our nede:
The king of Danmark with gret wrong
Thurth a geaunt that is so strong
2940 Wil strou al our thede.   *destroy; people (nation)*

"And whe han taken of him batayle   *we have agree to do combat with him*
On what maner, saunfayle,   *the nature of which, truly*
Y schal now tellen thee.
Thurth the bodi of a knight   *person*
2945 Ogains that geaunt to hold fight
Schal this lond aquite be.   *free (exempt from payment)*
And pilgrim for Him that dyed on Rode   *on [the] Cross*

	And that for ous schadde His blod	
	To bigge ous alle fre,	*save mankind*
2950	Take the batayle now on hond	
	And save ous the right of Inglond	*rightful ownership (entitlement)*
	For Seynt Charité."	

	"Do way, leve sir," seyd Gii,	*Enough, dear*
	"Icham an old man, a feble bodi;	
2955	Mi strengthe is fro me fare."	
	The king fel on knes to grounde	
	And crid him merci in that stounde	*moment*
	Yif it his wille ware,	
	And the barouns dede also,	
2960	O knes thai fellen alle tho	
	With sorwe and sikeing sare.	
	Sir Gii biheld the lordinges alle	
	And whiche sorwe hem was bifalle,	
	Sir Gii hadde of hem care.	*concern for them*

2965	Sir Gii tok up the king anon	*lifted up [to standing]*
	And bad the lordinges everichon	
	Thai schuld up stond,	
	And seyd, "For God in Trinité	
	And forto make Inglond fre	
2970	The batayle Y nim on hond."	*take*
	Than was the king ful glad and blithe	
	And thonked Gii a thousend sithe	*times*
	And Jhesu Cristes sond.	
	To the king of Danmark he sent than	
2975	And seyd he hadde founden a man	
	To fight for Inglond.	

	The Danismen busked hem yare	*prepared themselves quickly*
	Into batayle forto fare,	
	To fight thai war wel fawe.	*eager*
2980	And Gii was armed swithe wel	*exceedingly*
	In a gode hauberk of stiel	
	Wrought of the best lawe.	*Made in the best way*
	An helme he hadde of michel might	*strength*

107

With a cercle of gold that schon bright

2985 With precious stones on rawe.   *in a row*

In the frunt stode a charbukel ston   *carbuncle*

As bright as ani sonne it schon   *sun*

That glemes under schawe.   *in the dark*

On that helme stode a flour   *ornamental flower*

2990 Wrought it was of divers colour,   *various*

Mirie it was to bihold.   *Beautiful*

Trust and trewe was his ventayle   *face-guard*

Gloves and gambisoun and hosen of mayle   *jacket*

As gode knight have scholde;

2995 Girt he was with a gode brond   *Armed*

Wele kerveand biforn his hond;   *sharp-edged in*

A targe listed with gold   *shield bordered*

Portreyd with thre kinges corn   *Adorned; carved (engraved)*

That present God when He was born,   *offered [gifts to]*

3000 Mirier was non on mold.   *More beautiful; on earth*

And a swift-ernand stede   *fast-galloping*

Al wrin thai dede him lede,   *outfitted (equipped)*

His tire it was ful gay.   *attire; handsome*

Sir Gii opon that stede wond   *went (i.e., hoisted himself)*

3005 With a gode glaive in hond

And priked him forth his way.   *spurred*

And when he com to the plas

Ther the batayl loked was   *decreed*

Gii light withouten delay   *dismounted*

3010 And fel on knes doun in that stede

And to God he bad his bede   *prayed*

He schuld ben his help that day.

"Lord," seyd Gii, "that rered Lazeroun   *raised Lazarus*

And for man tholed passioun   *suffered death*

3015 And on the Rode gan blede,

That saved Sussan fram the feloun

And halp Daniel fram the lyoun,   *lion*

Today wisse me and rede.   *guide; advise*

Astow art mighti heven-king

3020	Today graunt me thi blisseing	
	And help me at this nede;	
	And Levedi Mari ful of might	*Lady*
	Today save Inglondes right	*rightful ownership*
	And leve me wele to spede."	*enable; attain success*
3025	When the folk was samned bi bothe side	*assembled*
	The to kinges with michel pride	*two; honor*
	After the relikes thai sende,	*holy relics*
	The corporas and the Messe gere.	*altar cloth; implements of Mass*
	On the halidom thai gun swere	*sacred relics*
3030	With wordes fre and hende.	
	The king of Danmarke swore furst, ywis,	
	Yif that his geant slayn is	
	To Danmarke he schal wende	*return*
	And never more Inglond cum withinne	
3035	No non after him of his kinne	
	Unto the warldes ende.	
	Sethen swore the king Athelston	*Afterwards*
	And seyd among hem everichon	
	Bi God that al may weld,	*rule*
3040	Yif his man ther slayn be	
	Or overcomen that men may se	
	Recreaunt in the feld,	*Defeated*
	His man he wil bicom an hond	*His (Anlaf's) vassal; assuredly*
	And alle the reme of Inglond	*realm*
3045	Of him forto helde	*submit*
	And hold him for lord and king	
	With gold and silver and other thing	
	Gret trowage him forto yelde.	*tribute; pay*
	When thai had sworn and ostage founde	*exchanged hostages as a guarantee*
3050	Colbrond stirt up in that stounde,	*leapt up*
	To fight he was ful felle.	*fierce*
	He was so michel and so unrede	*monstrous*
	That non hors might him lede	*carry*
	In gest as Y you telle.	
3055	So mani he hadde of armes gere	*fighting equipment*

	Unnethe a cart might hem bere	*Hardly*
	The Inglisse forto quelle.	*English man; kill*
	Swiche armour as he hadde opon,	
	Ywis, no herd ye never non	*you never heard of*
3060	Bot as it ware a fende of Helle.	*Unless it were; devil*

	Of mailes was nought his hauberk,	
	It was al of another werk	*kind of workmanship*
	That mervail is to here.	*astonishing; hear*
	Alle it were thicke splentes of stiel,	*plates*
3065	Thicke yjoined strong and wel,	*Tightly set together*
	To kepe that fendes fere.	*protect; devil's comrade*
	Hossen he hadde also wele ywrought	*leg-guards; well-made*
	Other than splentes was it nought	
	Fram his fot to his swere.[1]	
3070	He was so michel and so strong	
	And therto wonderliche long	*incredibly tall*
	In the world was non his pere.	*peer*

	An helme he hadde on his heved sett	*helmet*
	And therunder a thicke bacinet;	*subhelmet*
3075	Unsemly was his wede.	*Ugly*
	A targe he had wrought ful wel —	*shield*
	Other metel was ther non on bot stiel —	
	A michel and unrede.	*excessively large*
	Al his armour was blac as piche	*pitch*
3080	Wel foule he was and lothliche,	*ugly*
	A grisely gom to fede.	*terrible creature; nourish (sustain)*
	The heighe king that sitteth on heighe	
	That welt this warld fer and neighe	*rules*
	Made him wel ivel to spede.	*difficult to succeed over [in battle]*

3085	A dart he bar in his hond kerveand	*spear; sharp-pointed*
	And his wepen about him stondand	
	Bothe bihinde and biforn	
	Axes and gisarmes scharp ygrounde	*halberds; whetted*

---

[1] Lines 3068–69: *It was nothing but steel plates / From his foot to his neck*

110

	And glaives forto give with wounde	*spears*
3090	To hundred and mo ther worn.	*Two; were*
	The Inglis biheld him fast.	*English [spectators] stared intently at him*
	King Athelston was sore agast	*terrified*
	Inglond he schuld have lorn	
	For when Gii seighe that wicked hert	*heart*
3095	He nas never so sore aferd	*terribly afraid*
	Sethen that he was born.	*Since [the time]; (i.e., in all his life)*

	Sir Gii lepe on his stede fot-hot	
	And with a spere that wele bot	*cut*
	To him he gan to ride.	
3100	And he schet to Gii dartes thre,	*threw at*
	Of the tuay than failed he,	*With the [first] two he missed*
	The thridde he lete to him glide,	*third; shot to him [Guy]*
	Thurth Gyes scheld it glod	*pierced*
	And thurth his armour withouten abod	*without stopping*
3105	Bituene his arme and side	
	And quitelich into the feld it yede	*completely; went*
	The mountaunce of an acre brede	*distance; the width of an acre*
	Er that it wald abide.	*Before it would stop*

	Sir Gii to him gan to drive	
3110	That his spere brast afive	*broke into five pieces*
	On his scheld that was so bounde;	*ready*
	And Colbrond with michel hete	*fury*
	On Gyes helme he wald have smite,	*struck*
	And failed of him that stounde;	*But missed; moment*
3115	Bituix the sadel and the arsoun	*pommel*
	The strok of that feloun glod adoun	*cut down*
	Withouten wem or wounde.	*injury*
	That sadel and hors atuo he smot,	*cut in half*
	Into the erthe wele half a fot	
3120	And Gii fel doun to grounde.	

	Sir Gii as tite up stirt	*right away*
	As man that was agremed in hert,	*incensed*
	His stede he hadde forlore.	*lost*
	On his helme he wald hit him tho	

111

3125	Ac he no might nought reche therto	*reach*
	Bi to fot and yete more,	*two feet; still more*
	Bot on his schulder the swerd fel doun	
	And carf bothe plates and hauberjoun	*plate armor; jacket of mail*
	With his grimli gore.	*deadly weapon*
3130	Thurth al his armour stern and strong	
	He made him a wounde a spanne long	*hand's breadth*
	That greved him ful sore.	
	Colbrond was sore aschame	*ashamed*
	And smot Gii with michel grame.	*rage*
3135	On his helm he hit him tho	
	That his floures everichon	
	And his gode charbukel ston	
	Wel even he carf atuo.	*Completely; in two*
	Even ato he smot his scheld	
3140	That it fleyghe into the feld.	*flew*
	When Gii seyghe it was so	
	That he hadde his scheld forlorn,	
	Half bihinde and half biforn,	
	In hert him was wel wo.	
3145	And Gii hent his swerd an hond	*seized*
	And heteliche smot to Colbrond —	*fiercely*
	As a child he stode him under.	
	Open the scheld he yave him swiche a dent	*Upon*
	Bifor the stroke the fiir out went	*[sparks of] fire*
3150	As it were light of thonder.	*Like lightning from*
	The bondes of stiel he carf ichon	*bands*
	And into the scheld a fot and half on	*onward*
	With his swerd he smot asunder,	*cut to pieces*
	And with the out-braiding his swerd brast.	*pulling out [of the sword]; broke*
3155	Thei Gii were than sore agast	
	It was litel wonder.[1]	

---

[1] Lines 3155–56: *If Guy was then intensely afraid / It was no surprise*

Tho was Gii sore desmayd
And in his hert wel ivel ypayd   *unsatisfied*
For the chaunce him was bifalle,   *lot*
3160   And for he hadde lorn his gode brond   *lost*
And his stede opon the sond   *ground*
To our Levedi he gan calle.
Than gun the Danis ost   *began*
Ich puken other and make bost   *Each to nudge the other and brag*
3165   And seyd among hem alle,
"Now schal the Inglis be slain in feld;
Gret trouage Inglond schal ous yeld   *tribute*
And evermore ben our thral."   *slave*

"Now, sir knight," seyd Colbrond,
3170   "Thou hast lorn thi swerd in thine hond,
Thi scheld and eke thi stede.   *also*
Do now wele, yeld thee to me   *Do the right thing; surrender yourself*
And smertlich unarme thee;   *quickly*
Cri merci Y thee rede.
3175   And for thou art so douhti knight   *seeing that*
Thou durst ogain me held fight
To mi lord Y schal thee lede   *take*
And with him thou schalt acorded be,   *reconciled*
In his court he wil hold thee   *protect*
3180   And finde that thee is nede."   *supply what you need*

"Do way," seyd Gii, "therof speke nought.   *Enough of this*
Bi Him that al this world hath wrought   *created*
Ich hadde lever thou were anhong.   *hung*
Ac thou hast armes gret plenté,
3185   Ywis, thou most lene me   *give*
On of thine axes strong."
Colbrond swore bi Apolin,   *Apollo*
"Of al the wepen that is min   *weaponry*
Her schaltow non afong.   *none receive*
3190   Now thou wilt nought do bi mi rede
Thou schalt dye on ivel dede   *painful (miserable) death*
Er that it be ought long."

113

	When Gii herd him speke so	
	Al sone he gan him turn tho	*At once*
3195	And to his wepen he geth	*(i.e., Colbrond's) stash of weapons*
	Ther his axes stode bi hemselve;	
	He kept on with a wel gode helve	*took one; long handle*
	The best him thought he seth,	
	To Colbrond ogain he ran	
3200	And seyd, "Traitour," to him than,	
	"Thou schalt han ivel deth.	
	Now ich have of thi wepen plenté	
	Wherewith that Y may were me	*With which; defend myself*
	Right maugré al thin teth."[1]	

	Colbrond than with michel hete	*fury*
3205	On Gyes helme he wald have smite	
	With wel gret hert tene	*anger at heart*
	Ac he failed of his dint	*But; missed; blow*
	And the swerd into the erthe went	
3210	A fot and more, Y wene.	*believe*
	And with Colbrondes out-draught	*[axe] overextended*
	Sir Gii with ax a strok him raught	*struck*
	A wounde that was wele sene.	*clearly*
	So smertliche he smot to Colbrond	*quickly*
3215	That his right arme with alle the hond	
	He strok of quite and clene.	*cut off completely*

	When Colbrond feld him so smite	*felt himself*
	He was wel wroth ye may wel wite,	*know*
	He gan his swerd up fond	*thrust up*
3220	And in his left hond op it haf	*heaved*
	And Gii in the nek a strok him gaf	
	As he gan stoupe for the brond	*bent down*
	That his heved fro the bodi he smot	*severed*
	And into the erthe half a fot	
3225	Thurth grace of Godes sond.	*ordinance*
	Ded he feld the glotoun thare.	*slew*

---

[1] *Despite all your boasting (lit., in spite of your teeth)*

The Denis with sorwe and care   *Danish*
Thai dight hem out of lond.   *took themselves*

Blithe were the Inglis men ichon.   *Joyful*
3230   Erls, barouns, and King Athelston,
       Thai toke Sir Gii that tide
       And ladde him to Winchester toun
       With wel fair processioun
       Over al bi ich a side.
3235   For joie belles thai gun ring
       Te Deum laudamus thai gun sing
       And play and michel pride.
       Sir Gii unarmed him and was ful blithe;
       His sclavain he axed also swithe,   *pilgrim's garb; immediately*
3240   No lenger he nold abide.   *wait*

       "Sir pilgrim," than seyd the king,
       "Whennes thou art withouten lesing?   *From where*
       Thou art douhti of dede,
       For thurth douhtines of thin hond
3245   Thou hast saved al Inglond.
       God quite thee thi mede,   *May God reward you*
       And mi treuthe Y schal plight thee,   *pledge*
       So wele Y schal feffe thee   *endow*
       Bothe in lond and lede   *land and people*
3250   That of riches in toun and tour   *[So] that [in terms] of*
       Thou schalt be man of mest honour   *greatest glory*
       That woneth in al mi thede."   *lives; realm*

       "Sir King," seyd the pilgrim,
       "Of alle the lond that is tin   *yours*
3255   Y no kepe therof na mare   *desire; none of it*
       Bot now ichave the geant slain,
       Therof, ywis, icham ful fain,   *content*
       Mi way ichil forth fare."
       "Merci, sir," the king seyd than,
3260   "Tel me for Him that made man —
       For nothing thou ne spare —   *Do not hold back for any reason*
       Tel me what thi name it be,

115

Whennes thou art and of what cuntré
Or Y schal dye for care."   *concern*

3265 "Sir King," he seyd, "Y schal tel it thee.
      What mi right name it be
      Thou schalt witen anon;   *know at once*
      Ac thou schalt go with me yfere   *together*
      That no man of our conseyl here[1]
3270 Bot thou and Y alon."
      The king him graunted and was blithe,
      He comand his folk also swithe
      No wight with him to gon.   *person*
      Out of the toun than went he   *they*
3275 Wele half a mile fram that cité
      And ther made Gii his mon.   *entreaty*

      "Sir King," seyd Gii, "understond to me.
      O thing Y schal now pray thee   *One*
      Astow art curteys and hende:
3280 Yif Y mi name schal thee sayn
      That to no man thou no schalt me wrayn   *reveal*
      To this yere com to th'ende.   *until; the end*
      Gii of Warwike mi nam is right,   *truly*
      Whilom Y was thine owhen knight   *Once*
3285 And held me for thi frende;
      And now icham swiche astow may see.
      God of Heven biteche Y thee,
      Mi way Y wil forth wende."

      When the king seighe sikerly
3290 That it was the gode Gii
      That fro him wald his way   *would go*
      On knes he fel adoun to grounde,
      "Leve Sir Gii," in that stounde,   *Dear*
      "Merci," he gan to say.
3295 "For Godes love bileve with me   *remain*

_____

[1] *[So] that nobody is able to hear our private discussion*

116

And mi treuthe Y schal plight thee   *promise I will make you*
That Y schal this day
Sese and give into thine hond
Half the reme of Inglond;
3300   For Godes love say nought nay."

"Sir King," seyd Gii, "Y nil nought so.
Have thou thi lond for evermo
And God Y thee biteche;
Ac yif Herhaud to this lond com
3305   And bring with him Reynbroun mi sone
Help him Y thee biseche.   *entreat*
For thai er bothe hende and fre,
On Herhaud thou might trust thee
To take of thine fon wreche."   *take revenge on your enemies*
3310   Thai kisten hem togider tho
Al wepeand thai wenten ato   *weeping; separated*
Withouten ani more speche.

The king wel sore wepe for pité
And went him hom to his meyne   *household*
3315   With a mournand chere.   *grieving expression*
His folk ogaines him gan gon   *came to him*
And asked the king sone anon
What man the pilgrim were.
Thai seyd, "He is a douhti knight.
3320   Wald Jhesu ful of might
He wald leve with ous here."   *stay*
The king seyd, "Al stille ye be.   *be quiet*
What he is your non schal wite for me,   *none of you; from*
Iwis, of al this yere."   *for the duration of this year*

3325   Sir Gii went in his way forth right,   *immediately*
Oft he thonked God Almight
That the geaunt was slawe.
To Warwike he went to that cité
Ther he was lord of that cuntré
3330   To hold with right lawe.
He nas knowen ther of no man   *recognized*

117

When he to the castel gates cam,
Therof he was ful fawe.   *joyful*
Among the pouer men he him dede   *placed himself*
3335   Ther thai weren up in a stede   *one place*
And sett him on a rawe.   *sat himself among a group [of poor men]*

And Feliis the countas was ther than.   *countess*
In this warld was non better wiman,
In gest as so we rede,
3340   For thritten pouer men and yete mo   *thirteen*
For hir lordes love sche loved so,   *husband's*
Ich day sche gan fede
With than God and our Levedi   *In the hope that*
Schuld save hir lord Sir Gii   *protect*
3345   And help him at his nede.
Sche no stint noither day no night,   *did not cease [in her efforts]*
For him sche bisought God Almight   *(i.e., Guy)*
With bedes and almos dede.   *prayers; charitable works*

On a day the levedi went to mete   *dinner*
3350   And bad men schuld biforn hir fete   *requested; bring*
Hir pouer men al biden.   *all together*
And men brought hem everichon
And Gii of Warwike was that on   *one of them*
Of tho ich thritten.   *those same*
3355   In his hert he hadde gret care   *concern*
That he schuld be knawen thare
Of hem that hadde him sen;
Ac ther was non so wise of sight   *perceptive*
That him ther knowe might
3360   So misais he was and lene.   *wretched; thin*

The levedi biheld him inliche   *carefully*
Hou mesays he was sikerliche.   *poor; truly*
Curteys sche was and hende,
Of everich mete of everich dring   *food; drink*
3365   That sche ete of herself withouten lesing
Sche was him ful mende;   *[towards] him; thoughtful*
Of hire bere and of hir wine   *beer*

118

In hir gold coupe afine   *completely*
Oft sche gan him sende   *Repeatedly*
3370   And bad him ich day com he schold,
Mete and drink sche finde him wold
Unto his lives ende.

Sir Gii thonked that levedi oft   *many times*
Bot alle another was his thought   *quite different*
3375   Than he wald to hir say.   *Than [what] he would*
When the grace were yseyd
And the bordes adoun layd   *tables; set*
Out of toun he went his way.
Into a forest wenden he gan
3380   To an hermite he knewe er than   *previously*
To speke him yif he may.   *instruct*
And when he thider comen was
The gode hermite thurth Godes grace
Was dede and loken in clay.   *buried in the earth*

3385   Than thought Sir Gii anon   *decided*
That wald he never thennes gon   *from that place*
Therwhiles he war olive.
With a prest he spac of that cuntray   *priest*
That dede him Servise ich day   *Who performed Mass for him daily*
3390   And of his sinnes gan schrive.   *heard confession*
With him he hadde ther a page   *personal servant*
That served him in that hermitage
Withouten chest and strive.   *disagreement or disturbance*
No lenger was he lives there   *alive*
3395   Bot nighen monethes of a yere   *nine*
As ye may listen and lithe.   *listen and hear*

In slepe as Gii lay anight
God sent an angel bright
Fram Heven to him thare.
3400   "Gii," seyd the angel, "slepestow?   *[do] you sleep*
Hider me sent thee King Jhesu
To bid thee make thee yare,   *yourself ready*
For bi the eightenday at morwe   *eighth day (in a week)*

119

He schal deliver thee out of thi sorwe
3405 Out of this warld to fare.
To Heven thou schalt com Him to
And live with ous evermo
In joie withouten care."

When Gii was waked of that drem   *dream*
3410 Of an angel he seighe a glem.   *emanating radiance*
"What artow?" than seyd he.
The angel answerd, "Fram Heven Y cam,
Mighel is mi right nam.   *correct name*
God sent me to thee
3415 To bid thee make thee redi way,[1]
Bi the eightenday thou schalt day   *die*
Wel siker maughtow be.   *you can be certain*
And Y schal feche thi soule ful even   *quickly*
And bere it to the blis of Heven
3420 With grete solempneté."   *ceremony*

The angel goth forth and Gii bileft stille,   *remained*
His bedes he bad with gode wille   *prayers*
To Jhesu Heven-king.
And when his term was nere gon   *life's duration*
3425 His knave he cleped to him anon   *servant boy he called*
And seyd withouten lesing,
"Sone," he seyd, "Y pray now thee   *Boy*
Go to Warwike that cité
Withouten more duelling;   *delay*
3430 And when thou comest ther Y thee biseche
Gret wele the countas with thi speche
And take hir this gold ring.

"And say the pilgrim hat hir biforn   *who ate before her*
That hir mete was to born   *taken to*
3435 On the pouer mannes rawe,   *In the poor men's company*
Gret hir wele in al thing   *Greets; every way*

---

[1] *To tell you to prepare for yourself a direct passage [to Heaven]*

	And sende to hir this gold ring	*sends*
	Yif that sche wil it knawe.	*recognize*
	Als son as sche hath therof a sight	*of it*
3440	Sche wil it knawe anonright	*immediately*
	And be therof ful fawe.	*joyful*
	Than wil sche ax ware Y be.	
	Leve sone, for love of me,	*Dear boy*
	The sothe to hir thou schawe.	

	"And say icham for Godes love	
3445	In the forest hermite bicome	
	Mine sinnes forto bete;	*atone*
	And bid hir for the love of me	
	That sche com hider with thee	*here*
3450	For nothing sche no lete.	*delay*
	And when ye com ye finde me dede	*If*
	Do me never hennes lede	
	Bot grave me here in grete.[1]	
	And after sche schal dye, ywis,	
3455	And com to me into Heven-blis	
	Ther joies her ful swete."	*There; [to] hear; dulcet*

	The knave went forth anon,	
	Into Warwike he gan gon	
	Bifor that levedi fre.	
3460	And when he hadde that levedi founde	
	On knes he fel adoun to grounde	
	And seyd, "Listen to me,	
	The pilgrim that ete thee biforn	
	That thi mete was to born	
3465	An hermite now is he.	
	He greteth thee wele in al thing	
	And sent thee this gold ring	
	In sum tokening to be."	*As some authentication*

---

[1] Lines 3452–53: *Never transport me from here / But bury me here in the earth*

	The levedi tok that ring an hond	*in her hand*
3470	And loked theron and gan withstond	*paused*
	The letters forto rede.	
	"Ow, certes," quath the levedi,	*Oh, truly*
	"This ring Y gaf mi lord Sir Gii	
	When he fro me yede."	
3475	For sorwe sche fel aswon, ywis,	
	And when that sche arisen is	
	To the knave sche gan spede.	
	"Leve sone," sche seyd, "Y pray thee	
	Wher is that pilgrim telle thou me	
3480	And gold schal be thi mede."	*reward*

	"Madame," seyd the knave ful skete,	*quickly*
	"In the forest ichim lete,	*I left him*
	Right now Y com him fro.	
	He is ner ded in the hermitage,	
3485	On his halve Y make the message;	*behalf*
	Ywis, he bad me so	
	And bad thou schust to him come,	
	For that ich trewe love	*same*
	That was bituene you tuo	
3490	Do him never lede oway	
	Bot biri him right ther in clay,	
	Olive sestow him no mo."	*you will see him*

	The levedi was glad of that tiding	
	And thonked Jhesu Heven-king	
3495	And was in hert ful blithe	
	That sche schuld sen hir lord Sir Gii;	
	Ac for o thing sche was sori	
	That he schuld dye so swithe.	
	Thai made hem redi forto wende	*themselves; depart*
3500	With knightes and with levedis hende.	*gracious*
	On a mule thai sett hir sithe	*then*
	And with al the best of that cité	*finest (highest in rank)*
	To th'ermitage went sche	*the hermitage*
	As ye may listen and lithe.	*hear*

3505	To th'ermitage when thai come
	Ther thai light al and some *dismounted*
	And in sche went wel even. *directly*
	When that sche seighe hir lord Sir Gii
	Sche wept and made doleful cri
3510	With a ful reweful steven. *voice*
	Sir Gii loked on hir thare,
	His soule fram the bodi gan fare.
	A thousand angels and seven
	Underfenge the soule of Gii *Received*
3515	And bar it with gret molodi
	Into the blis of Heven.

Than was that levedi ful of care
For hir lord was fram hir fare, *gone*
"Allas!" it was hir song.
3520 Sche kist his mouthe, his chin also,
And wepe with hir eighen to *two eyes*
And hir hondes sche wrong.
Gret honour dede our Lord for Gii:
A swete brathe com fram his bodi *fragrant breath*
3525 That last that day so long *lasted*
That in this world spices alle *aromatic spices*
No might cast a swetter smalle *smell*
As then was hem among.

The levedy as tite dede send hir sond *right away; summons*
3530 After bischopes, abotes of the lond,
The best that might be founde, *highest ranking*
And when thider was com that fair ferred *company [of people]*
To Warwike thai wald him lede *wanted to take [Guy]*
As lord of michel mounde. *importance*
3535 Bot al the folk that ther was
No might him stir of that plas *were not able to move him*
Ther he lay on the grounde.
An hundred men about him were
No might him nought thennes bere
3540 For hevihed that stounde. *heaviness*

Than seyd the levedi, "Lete him be stille;
Never more remoun him Y nille   *remove; will not*
No do him hennes lede.   *cause him to be moved hence*
He sent me bode with his page   *command*
3545   To biri him in this hermitage
Simpliche withouten prede."   *ostentation*
Thay tok a through of marbel ston   *marble container (trough)*
And leyd his bodi therin anon
Atird in knightes wede.
3550   Fair servise than was thare   *religious service*
Of bischopes, abbotes that ther ware,
And clerkes to sing and rede.

When thai hadde birid his bodi anon,
The gret lordinges everichon
3555   Hom thai gun wende,
Ac the levedi left stille thare;   *remained*
Sche nold never thennes fare,
Sche kidde that sche was kende.   *showed; dutiful (loving)*
Sche lived no lenger sothe to say
3560   Bot right on the fiftenday   *fifteenth day*
Sche dyed that levedi hende
And was birid hir lord by   *beside*
And now thai er togider in compeynie   *are*
In joie that never schal ende.

3565   When Sir Tirri herd telle this
That Gii his fere ded is   *friend*
And birid in the clay,
He com to this lond withouten lesing
And bisought Athelston the king
3570   His bodi to leden oway.
He it graunted him ful yare,
Into Lorain with him gan fare
Into his owhen cuntray.
An abbay he lete make tho   *had made there*
3575   Forto sing for hem to   *two [Guy and Felice]*
Ever more til Domesday.   *the Last Judgment*

Now have ye herd lordinges of Gii
That in his time was so hardi
And holden hende and fre,
3580 And ever he loved treuthe and right   *loyalty; justice*
And served God with al his might
That sit in Trinité.
And therfore at his ending-day
He went to the joie that lasteth ay
3585 And evermore schal be.
Now God leve ous to live so   *enable*
That we may that joie com to.
Amen, par charité.

Explanatory Notes

1–24   As the Middle English redactor selected a tranche of material from midway through his source *Gui de Warewic*, a certain amount of editorial shaping was necessary at various narrative junctures. Here, at the opening of the romance, the conventional laudatory description of the protagonist has been extended to include a recapitulation that summarizes events from the earlier part of Guy's life. These first two stanzas are not included in *Gui de Warewic* but were added by the Middle English redactor in order to orient the narrative and to signal, in the traditional manner, the opening of a new romance. The final stanza was, likewise, added by the Middle English redactor to mark narrative closure. For a discussion of the redactor's omission of the "Reinbroun" material, see the note to lines 1843–44.

1–3   *God graunt hem heven-blis to mede / That herken to mi romaunce rede / Al of a gentil knight.* As is typical of romance, an oral storytelling context is imagined. This opening stanza contains a number of traditional elements: a prayer for the audience, a statement of subject, and praise for the hero. The narrator's call to an audience to "listen" to his romance being "read" aloud is suggestive of the affiliations of romance with both orality and literacy in terms of origins, composition, and transmission. The opinions of commentators vary as to the relative extent to which orality and literacy should each be regarded as influential. For a range of views on this issue see: Albert C. Baugh, "The Middle English Romance: Some Questions of Creation, Presentation, and Preservation" (*Speculum* 42 [1967], 1–31); M. Chesnutt, "Minstrel Reciters and the Enigma of the Middle English Romance" (*Culture and History* 2 [1987], 48–67); Ruth Crosby, "Oral Delivery in the Middle Ages" (*Speculum* 11 [1936], 88–110); Andrew Taylor, "Fragmentation, Corruption, and Minstrel Narration: The Question of the Middle English Romances" (*Yearbook of English Studies* 22 [1992], 38–62).

12–13   *Of Warwike wise and wight. / Wight he was for sothe to say.* The repetition of "wight" links the end of one stanza and the start of the next. This use of repetition has an obvious structural function and can be compared with certain forms of "catenation" in Anglo-Norman *chansons de geste*, where they are accounted for as memorial aids for the oral reciter. Similar structural repetitions appear elsewhere in the stanzaic *Guy of Warwick*. For example, Guy's parting speech to Felice begins with his address to her as "Leve leman" and this is echoed as "Leman" four more times during the speech, each at the start or mid-point of a stanza (lines 337, 349, 361, 373, 379). For further discussion of the use of this and similar kinds of repetitions in romance, see Smithers (1988), pp. 192–94.

20   *Athelston.* The Saxon King Athelstan ruled 924–39 and is best known for his defeat of the Scots and Danes at the Battle of Brunanburh in 937. This battle, recorded in the Anglo-Saxon Chronicle and sung as a great victory won by Athelstan over the Viking invader Anlaf, is traditionally said to have inspired the story of Guy and Colbrond that appears in the *Stanzaic Guy of Warwick* lines 2965–3324; see Legge (1963), p. 162. The location of the battle near Winchester is not that of the historical event and the romance does not attempt an accurate historical presentation. Nevertheless, the historicity of the *Stanzaic Guy of Warwick* is important to its meaning, and Field (p. 168) and Klausner (p. 117) each argue that the historical setting is essential to its success. There are a number of indications that the historicity of *Guy of Warwick* informed its contemporary reception and from the early fourteenth century Guy is mentioned in chronicle accounts of Athelstan's reign. The *Short Metrical Chronicle*, for example, concludes its account of Athelstan's reign with a description of how:

> In Aþelstonis time, ich understond,
> Was Gii of Warwike in Inglond
> & for Aþelston he dede a bateyle
> Wiþ a geaunt gret, saunfaile.
> Þe geaunt hiȝt Colbro[n]d,
> Gy him slouȝ wiþ his hond.
> At Winchester þe bataile was don
> & seþþe dede Gii never non. (lines 1663–70)

Guy's battle with Colbrond is also included in the account of Athelstan's reign in Peter Langtoft's *Chronique d'Angleterre*, c. 1306, translated into English by Robert Mannyng c. 1338. Langtoft directly associates Guy's legendary battle with the Battle of Brunanburh in order to forge a parallel with Edward I's battles with the Scots, one which would suggest, by historical and legendary association, the chivalrous status of Edward's own military accomplishments. For further discussion of these chronicle accounts, see Richmond, pp. 65–76.

22–24   *For his love ich understond / He slough a dragoun in Northhumberlond / Ful fer in the north cuntré.* The dragon-slaying episode from Guy's youth is recounted in other versions of the romance and is the concluding episode of the couplet *Guy of Warwick* (lines 7141–7306). The episode is also referred to in *Bevis of Hampton*, where the narrator includes Guy in a list of great heroes of romance: "And Gy a Warwik, ich understonde, / Slough a dragoun in North Homberlonde" (lines 2607–08). The reference suggests this was a particularly well-known episode, though the similarity of phrasing with the stanzaic *Guy* may imply that one of these references was based upon the other.

71   *Other lord nil Y non take.* Double negatives are common in Middle English and invariably function to add emphasis; they do not cancel each other out.

75   *That semly was of sight.* The expression "of sight" has the sense "to be seen," "as can be seen," or "in appearance," and occurs six times elsewhere in the text, always in the tail-rhyme position (lines 675, 909, 1128, 1776, 2292, 2832). It is formulaic and appears in other romances with this sense, for example, *The King of Tars*: "Þat grimli was of siȝt" (line 168); *Reinbroun*: "Þo child so faire of siȝt" and "Grisliche he was of siȝte" (stanza 8, line 2, and stanza 34, line 12); *Amis and Amiloun*: "Tho gomes, that were egre of sight" (line 1309).

97–102   *Felice answerd ogain . . . / Bi Him that schop mankende.* The awkwardness here, which is a kind of periphrasis, reflects the Middle English redactor's attempt to compress what were in the couplet source two distinct statements from Felice:

> "Sire," fait ele, "jo en penserai,
> De ci al tirerz jur le vus dirrai."
> Cum il vint al tierz jur,
> Li quons apele par grant amur
> Felice sa fille qui tant ert sage:
> "Fille, di mei tun corage."
> "Sire," fait ele, "ben vus mustrai
> Cum en mun corage proposé l'ai;
> Ne vus en peist si jol vus di,
> Bel dulz sire, ço vus en pri." (*Gui de Warewic*, lines 7461–70)

Mills (1991), p. 227, comments that, as a result of the omission of lines 7464–66, "the heroine now seems to be clearing her throat at somewhat excessive length, giving a (nervous?) hiccough in the middle of doing so, and starting again from the beginning. None of which is really like her at all."

123   *Sir Gii the conquerour.* The title "conqueror" denotes a victorious ruler and in contemporary texts tends to be applied to historical figures. "King Richard" and

"Charls" are both referred to as "þe conquerour" in the romances *Richard Coer de Lyon* (line 1015) and *Roland and Vernague* (line 57; in *The Taill of Rauf Coilyear, with the Fragments of Roland and Vernagu and Otuel*, ed. Sidney J. H. Herrtage, EETS e.s. 39 [London: N. Trübner and Co., 1882; rpt. H. Milford, 1931]); Robert Mannying refers in his chronicle to "William conqueroure" (chapter 2, lines 2122, 4455, 4564); and the *Cursor Mundi* refers to "Alisaunder þe conquerour" (line 3, ed. Richard Morris, 7 vols., EETS o.s. 57, 59, 62, 66, 68, 99, 101 [London: K. Paul, Trench, Trübner, and Co., 1874; rpt. London: Oxford University Press, 1961]).

128–29   *Tel me the sothe par charité / Y pray thee, par amoure.* This case of periphrasis, which results in the earl's excessive politeness, occurred during translation and can be compared to lines 97–102 above.

169–216   Significant interest has been generated in the relationship between these four stanzas and similar descriptions of feasting in *Amis and Amiloun*, another East Midland tail-rhyme romance from the Auchinleck MS. The comparable passages occur in *Amis and Amiloun* at lines 97–132, 409–44, and 1505–24. Particularly close similarities can be observed by comparing lines 181–83, 190–91, 195, and 211–13 from the stanzaic *Guy of Warwick* with the following passage from *Amis and Amiloun*:

> Fourtennight, as me was told,
> With meet and drynke, meryst on mold
> To glad the bernes blithe;
> Ther was mirthe and melodye
> And al maner of menstracie
> Her craftes for to kithe;
> Opon the fiftenday ful yare
> Thai token her leve forto fare
> And thonked him mani a sithe. (lines 100–08)

Loomis (pp. 613–27) and Fewster (pp. 60–66) each suppose that *Amis and Amiloun* was derived from the stanzaic *Guy*. However, the subsequent consideration by Mills (1991), who gives *Amis* priority, seems the most convincing. Mills argues that here, as at other points, the Middle English redactor of the stanzaic *Guy* had loosely followed *Gui de Warewic* but used his knowledge of *Amis and Amiloun* in order to amplify and re-structure his material into stanza form.

190–210   *Ther was mirthe and melody.* References to professional entertainers are common in metrical romance and appear in such diverse specimens of the genre as *Emaré* (line 13), *Sir Orfeo* (line 449), *Sir Gowther* (line 531), *Sir Cleges* (line 99), *William of Palerne* (line 5355), *The Seege or Batayle of Troye* (line 804), and *Kyng Alisaunder* (line 5981). The description here in the *Stanzaic Guy of Warwick* is comprised of several conventional elements; the statement that there was "every kind of entertainment" is typical, as is the listing of instruments and reference to singers or tale tellers. What is unusual is the length and detail of this description. Not only are several elements combined but these are repeated and extended, so an unusually long list of seven instruments is given (there are players on horns, drums, fiddle, crowd, harp, organs, bagpipes) and the narrator asserts that there is *al maner menstracie* (line 191) and then, again, that there is *al maner of gle* (line 202). See also the note to line 197, below.

194   *croude.* The *croude* was a straight-sided, six-stringed instrument of Welsh origin that was plucked or played with a bow. For a full description see Otto Emanuel Andersson, *The Bowed-Harp: A Study in the History of Early Musical Instruments*, trans. Mary Stenbäck, ed. and trans. Kathleen Schlesinger (London: W. Reeves, 1930), pp. 195ff.

197   *Minstrels of mouthe and mani dysour.* References to singers or tale tellers appear in several other romances: *Kyng Alisaunder* (line 6981), *Firumbras* (line 417; in *Firumbras and Otuel and Roland*, ed. Mary Isabelle O'Sullivan, EETS o.s. 198 [London: Oxford University Press, 1935]), and *The Seege or Batayle of Troye* (line 806) each refer to "dysoures" who "talen" or "synge and . . . carpe." However, it is difficult to be certain about exactly the kind of entertainment that is here being referred to. The *minstrels of mouthe* may be storytellers or singers. The term *dysour* may specify a storyteller but also seems to have been used as a more generalized term to refer to a range of different types of entertainers or jesters. See also the note to lines 190–210, above.

201   *to mithe.* The form is recorded nowhere else by the *MED*.

208–10   *Thai goven glewemen for her gle / Robes riche, gold and fe, / Her giftes were nought gnede.* The depiction of the patronage of entertainers is a topos found in a number of romances. The protagonists of *Sir Isumbras* (lines 19–21) and *Sir Cleges* (lines 37–48) are each lauded for their generosity towards minstrels, and *Sir Orfeo* pivots upon the fairy king's promise to repay the musician Orfeo "largelich" for his harping (line 451). There is a certain degree of correspondence here with the contemporary treatment of entertainers. The accounts of Thomas Lancaster show that in 1319 high-quality cloths were purchased for household musicians at the large sum of £13. Records of this type imply that skilled entertainers were often regarded as servants of status and rewarded accordingly. Such gift-giving also reflects the position of minstrels and musicians. Many were often only loosely connected to a parent household. As they therefore did not draw the same daily benefits as other servants, they would be recompensed on a more *ad hoc* basis. For further consideration of the position of minstrels and entertainers within the great household, see Woolgar, pp. 27–29.

216   *In gest also we rede.* In the stanzaic *Guy*, interjections from the narrator are of three main kinds: those which begin "In gest . . ." (". . . also we read" [line 216], ". . . as Y you say" [line 420], ". . . as Y you telle" [line 3054, etc.]); those which alliterate on "telle," "tale," "tong" ("no tong may telle in tale" [line 199], "With tong as Y thee telle" [line 741, etc.]); and those with "listen" ("listen and lithe" [line 3396], "listen and lere" [line 518], "listen now to me" [line 2192, etc.]). In addition, there are a number of very short phrases which represent interjections from the narrator and typically offer enforcement or claim the authority or truth of a statement, such as, "for sothe to say" (line 13), "ich understond" (line 22), "ich wene" (line 1611), "sikerly" (line 2779), and "verrament" (line 953).

234   *On hunting thai gun ride. On* is used before the verb to indicate an ongoing, continuous action; so, they continued to hunt regularly.

237   *In herd is nought to hide.* This expression also occurs in the tail-rhyme position in line 57 of *Sir Launfal* where Sands describes it as "One of many metrical expletives in *Launfal*, this one best rendered as 'No reason to hide anything'" (*Middle English Verse Romances* [Exeter: Exeter University Press, 1966], p. 205). It occurs eight times in the Auchinleck MS and always in the tail-rhyme position of texts written in twelve-line tail-rhyme stanzas: *Sir Owain* (line 420, in *Three Purgatory Poems*, ed. Edward E. Foster [Kalamazoo, MI: Medieval Institute Publications, 2004]), *Amis and Amiloun* (line 501), and *Horn Childe and Maiden Rimnild* (lines 39, 57, 189, 396, 669, and 729).

250   *with wrong.* The specific sense "sinfully" is implied; that is, "contrary to moral or religious teachings, wickedly; in a sinful or an immoral manner" (*MED*).

251   *it was his song.* A conventional expression with the sense that "all his speech" or "everything he said" was of this nature.

257–58   *For Him that bar the croun of thorn / Gode dede dede Y nare.* In Middle English
          romance, oaths and expressions that call upon God tend to be highly formulaic
          and, as here, a preference is shown for periphrastic forms. This example conforms
          to a pattern used repeatedly in the stanzaic *Guy*: periphrastic pious exclamations
          are typically of one line, begin with a version of "For Him that" (see also "Bi Him
          that," "To Him that," "Now God that" at lines 63, 333, and 1978) and end with
          a phrase which refers to the Creation (". . . schope mankinne," ". . . schope
          mankende," ". . . schope al mankinde" at lines 63, 333, and 1978) or the Passion
          (". . . this warld wan," ". . . suffred ded," ". . . schadde for ous His blod," ". . .
          dyed on Rode," "schadde His blod" at lines 134, 924, 2027, 2947, and 2948).
          Dalrymple (2000), pp. 123–26, counts twenty-seven pious formulae in the stan-
          zaic *Guy* and observes that images of the Passion are specifically invoked "when
          Guy speaks of his desire to appease God." He argues that they function to stress
          Guy's pious motives and would potentially have affective power upon read-
          ers/auditors who knew of their poignant use in other texts and were familiar with
          visual images of the Crucifixion. See the note to lines 1216–17 for a discussion
          of pious expressions which invoke the omnipotent Deity rather than the Passion.

331   *Chirches and abbays thou might make.* The endowment of religious foundations
          was common practice in the Middle Ages. In at least three other romances, unlike
          Guy, the protagonist does go ahead and build an abbey in order to win spiritual
          reward of some kind. The Northern *Octavian* recounts the story of a couple who
          cannot conceive a child so build an abbey to request intercession from Virgin; *Sir
          Gawain and the Carle of Carlisle* (in *Sir Gawain: Eleven Romances and Tales*,
          ed. Thomas Hahn [Kalamazoo, MI: Medieval Institute Publications, 1995]) tells
          how a man builds an abbey so that masses may be said for the men he has slain;
          in *Sir Gowther*, an abbey and convent are founded in penitence.

383   *And bothe thai fel aswon tho.* In the romance mode, the expression of emotion is
          signalled through a highly conventionalized pattern of gestures. Fainting (and
          sometimes the simultaneous fainting of two or more characters) may occur at
          moments of intense sorrow, as here. It may also follow a shock (as occurs when
          Guy reveals his identity to Tirri, lines 2699–2703) or indicate a general sense of
          being overwhelmed with emotion (such as when Felice breaks the news of Guy's
          departure, line 431). Other gestures representative of sorrow include sighing (line
          2787), going pale (line 2724), weeping (especially at parting, see lines 1679,
          2774, 3313), and crying "alas" or "wayleway" (lines 1708, 3519). Distress is also
          indicated by wringing hands (line 3522), tearing hair or clothes (line 544). See the

note to line 808 for a discussion of the significance of kisses exchanged between men.

388–93   *"Leman," sche seyd, "have here this ring . . . / And God Y thee betiche."* The ring given by Felice to Guy is a symbol of their relationship. It ultimately becomes a token of recognition when it is later returned by Guy to Felice (lines 3430–32 and 3467–74), at which point we also learn that it is a "gold" ring (line 3432) engraved with distinguishing "letters" (line 3471). Rings given on parting or as tokens of recognition are commonplace in romance tradition and appear, for example, in *King Horn* (lines 567–70, where the ring is also engraved), *Sir Perceval of Galles* (lines 471–74; in *Sir Perceval of Galles and Ywain and Gawain*, ed. Mary Flowers Braswell [Kalamazoo, MI: Medieval Institute Publications, 1999]), and *Sir Eglamour* (line 709).

397–408   This stanza offers a significantly abbreviated version of the Anglo-Norman source. *Gui de Warewic* (lines 7727–52) includes a description of how Guy leaves in secret for the Holy Land and his motivations (lines 7732–36: "En Jerusalem puis aler voldra. / Desore d'errer ne finera, / En Jerusalem si vendra / E en meinte estrange terre / U les sainz Deu purra requere" ["He desired then to go to Jerusalem. Henceforth, he will not cease from wandering until, by way of many strange lands, he reaches Jerusalem where he will be able to visit God's holy relics"]) as well as the actual words of Felice's lament. Observing this, Mills (1991), p. 224, comments that "Given the translator's weakness for producing whole stanzas that described wanderings over the face of England, Europe, or the Near East [see the notes to lines 469–80 and 829–40], it is at first surprising that he should not here have produced another wholly given up to Guy's pilgrimage." Mills' explanation is that the Middle English redactor was influenced by his knowledge of *Amis and Amiloun*, another twelve-line tail-rhyme romance, and had re-worked the couplet source into stanza form using *Amis* lines 253–64 as a model or "mould."

468   *With his brother Tirry.* Guy and Tirri are brothers in the sense of "sworn brothers," bound to each other by an oath of loyalty and brotherhood. They are close friends and comrades in arms although not blood relations. Their relationship is developed through the series of adventures they share together during Guy's youth. A specific episode in the couplet *Guy of Warwick* recounts the moment they make their bond of brotherhood:

Gii seyd to Tirry, wiþouten lesing:
"Ich wil þat we be treuþe-pliȝt

& sworn breþer anon riʒt,
Tirri," seyd sir Gyoun,
"Understond now to mi resoun
Þat noiþer oþer after þis
No faile oþer while he lives is."
Wiþ þat answerd þerl Tirri,
& seyd, "wel bleþelich, sir Gii.
Now þou lovest so miche me,
Þat tow mi sworn broþer wil be,
No wille ich never feyle þe
For nouʒt þat mai bifalle me.
Gret worþschip þou hast don me:
God leve me ʒete þan day yse
Þat ich it þe mow wele ʒeld.
For gode baroun þou art yheld;
Fram deþ þou hast ywarist me;
Wel gret wrong it schuld be
Bot ich þe loved as mi lord fre.
Wel gret worþschip ich ouʒt bere þe."
Treuþe bitven hem is pliʒt,
& after kist anonriʒt. (lines 4906–28)

For a discussion of the importance of the theme of sworn brotherhood in *Amis and Amiloun* and *Athelston* see the introductions to those texts in Foster and Herzman et al. A wide-ranging study of the topic is provided by John Boswell, *Same Sex Unions in Pre-Modern Europe* (New York: Villard Books, 1994).

469–80   *Menssangers anon thai sende . . . / Bi north no bi southe*. What is, in the Anglo-Norman source, a very short list of geographical names has here been expanded to a much longer catalogue. *Gui de Warewic* has: "Puis unt lur messages pris, / Par tote la terre l'unt il quis. / Mais quant pas trové ne l'unt, / Arere repairé se sunt" (lines 7815–18). Mills (1991), p. 220, cites this as an example of the Middle English redactor's tendency to amplify material from his source in order to make distinct sections fit the twelve lines of the stanza form. However, the expansion of another list of geographical names at lines 829–40 implies a particular interest in depictions of wandering (which is discussed in more detail above, in the Introduction, pp. 9–10). Smithers (p. 22) describes a comparable example of amplification in his edition of *Kyng Alisaunder*.

484   *Palmers wede*. Medieval pilgrims were identifiable by their characteristic *sclavin* ("cloak"), *scrip* ("bag" or "satchel"), and *burdoun* ("staff"). For a discussion of

the importance of recognizability and the potential advantages it offered pilgrims, see A. M. Koldeweij, "Lifting the Veil on Pilgrim Badges" in Stopford, pp. 161–88.

496   *He yede over alle bi doun and dale.* Compare to Chaucer's Tale of Sir Thopas, line 796: "By dale and eek by downe"; and *Sir Tryamour*, line 270: "Be dale and eke be downe."

517–19   *Now herken and ye may here / In gest yif ye wil listen and lere / Hou Gii as pilgrim yede.* This is an example of *transitio*, a rhetorical device whereby the narrator makes an explicit shift from the experiences of one character to another. It is a common procedure in Middle English verse narratives, Old French romance, and *chansons de geste*. For a detailed discussion of the use of such rhetorical devises in romance, see Smithers (1988), pp. 209–10.

541   Up until this point, the redactor has used the four-rhyme version of the twelve-line tail-rhyme stanza: *aabaabccbddb*. This version is unusual within the corpus of tail-rhyme romances and is only used consistently in *The King of Tars* and *Amis and Amiloun*. Mills (1991), p. 216, highlights the possibilities of this stanza form: "Its densely asymmetrical rhyme-structure encourages some distinctive narrative procedures and produces some particular dramatic effects; its first half tends to be relatively self-contained, involuted, static; its second, both more varied in content and more dynamic in impetus." As a result of the greater number of rhymes, this scheme is more demanding than the more common five-rhyme pattern (*aabccbddbeeb*) and, after alternating between the two from lines 541–624, the redactor settles on the five-rhyme pattern with only a few exceptions.

592   *Sarrayins.* The term "Saracen" has both generalized and more specific usages in Middle English. Here it refers to an Arab or Muslim, though elsewhere in romance, such as in *King Horn*, it may be used in a generalized way to refer to any non-Christian or opponent of Christianity.

619–24   *In a brom feld ther wer hidde . . . / And drof ous alle to schond.* An incident involving hiding in a field full of broom also occurs in *Kyng Alisaunder*: "He was hyd in lynde and brome" (line 2488).

638   *That we might to raunsoun come.* This refers to the practice of ransoming noblemen from the field. A well-known example is of Geoffrey Chaucer who,

when captured by the French during the Hundred Years War, was ransomed for £16. The regulation of this chivalric practice relied upon the importance of bonds between those of the same social rank (which existed even between opponents) and the potential for financial and personal advancement to be gained among the captors. See the discussion in Derek Pearsall, *The Life of Geoffrey Chaucer: A Critical Biography* (Oxford: Blackwell, 1992), pp. 40–46.

668   *Yif he wald ate ches playn.* Chess was a game associated with high culture and, as a war game, with chivalry. It was probably invented in India in the sixth century and over time spread to Western Europe, given impetus by the contact of the crusades with Islamic countries.

723   *parlement.* A council of nobles convened to advise and make a decision as a court of law.

734–35 *Have he Cristes curs and mine / With boke and eke with belle.* During the ceremony of excommunication in the Catholic Church a bell is rung, a book closed, and a candle extinguished to signify symbolically that, from that moment, the person is excluded from taking the sacraments and joining in divine worship.

752   *playn place.* A piece of flat, open ground designated for martial games (tournaments, jousts) and fighting.

777   *bond.* A serf or customary tenant (as distinct from a free-holder): "a villager (villain) or farmer (husbandman) holding land under a lord in return for customary services, esp[ecially] ploughing" (*MED*).

791   *burjays.* "A freeman of a town, a citizen with full rights and privileges" (*MED*).

808   *He kist me so glad he was.* Kissing and embracing between men is common in romance and has various significances. According to the encoded pattern of gestures, a kiss may be used to represent a strong feeling of happiness or given as a formal sign of reconciliation and restored friendship (line 2605). Both of these senses, joy and reconciliation, are implied by the kiss Triamour gives to Jonas. In cases of reconciliation where forgiveness or acquittal are specifically implied, then an embrace (initiated by the one who is forgiving or acquitting) rather than or as well as a kiss is given (as at lines 1609–14 and 2721). Kisses are also given at the parting of someone dear, as at line 1678 where Jonas and all his fifteen sons line up to kiss Guy good-bye. Gratitude and thanks are expressed by the kissing

of feet (lines 929–30). See the note to line 383 for discussion of the significance of other kinds of gestures in romance.

829–40   *Y sought hem into the lond of Coyne . . . / And thurthout al Breteyne.* Here, as at lines 469–80, what appears in the Anglo-Norman source as a brief list of names has been amplified by the Middle English redactor to become a much more extensive geographical itinerary. *Gui de Warewic* (lines 8135–38) has: "Dreit m'en alai en Alemaigne, / En Loheregne e en Espaigne, / E en Puille e en Sessoigne, / E en France e en Burgoigne" ["I went directly to Germany, to Lorraine and to Spain, and into Apulia and to Saxony, and to France and to Burgundy"].

983–85   *He slough mi brother Helmadan, / Thurth him icham forlore. / Min em he slough, the riche Soudan.* According to the couplet *Guy of Warwick* (lines 2947–52), it is not Guy but one of his comrades, Tebaud, who slew Helmadan. This episode and the slaying of the Sultan occur during Guy's exploits around Constantinople fighting for the Emperor Hernis. A similar reference to an episode in Guy's youth is subsequently made by Amorant (lines 1327–41).

1004–06   *Whi artow thus ivel ydight / And in thus pouer wede? / A feble lord thou servest, so thenketh me.* Triamour refers to the practice whereby knights and retainers were clothed and fed by their lord. The episode can be compared to one in *Sir Launfal* (lines 154–56) in which the appearance of Hugh and John, who return to Arthur's court very tattered and in the same clothes they left a year before, instantly prompts questions and speculation about their retaining lord during their time away.

1010–20   *A wel gode Lord than serve Y . . . / And live with joie and game.* Guy maintains his anonymity without lying about his situation by using the knight and his retaining lord as a metaphor for himself and his relationship with God. The metaphor is informed by the wider theme in the text of the "pilgrimage of life" and, as on other occasions, the disguise motif offers significant opportunity for dramatic irony.

1048   *Inde that cité.* See Index of Place Names.

1074   *stithe on stede.* "Powerful on horse." Compare *Sir Tristram* (in *Sir Tristram and Sir Lancelot of the Laik*, ed. Alan Lupack [Kalamazoo, MI: Medieval Institute Publications, 1994]), "With knightes stithe on stedes" (line 66) and *Sir Amadace*, "so stithe on stede" (line 577).

1076   *Espire*. Compare *Gui de Warewic*, line 8384, "Perse" (i.e., Persia).

1081–1119   This description provides a heroic genealogy for each item of armor given to Guy by Triamour. *King Clarel* (line 1085), who owned the hauberk, is the Saracen king and opponent of Charlemagne who features prominently in the Auchinleck MS romance *Otuel*. Clarel is imprisoned by Charlemagne's knights, then, when freed, takes Ogier prisoner before being slain by Otuel in hand-to-hand combat. *Alisaunder* (line 1102), who is said to have worn the helmet when he fought against *Poreus* (line 1103), is Alexander the Great, king of Macedonia, conqueror of the Persian empire (356–23 BC), and renowned hero of romance. The romance *Kyng Alisaunder* describes Alexander's pursuit of King Porus into India and how he forces him to become his subject and guide around the sub-continent; when Porus renounces his allegiance, Alexander slays him in single combat and assumes dominance over India. *King Darri* (line 1118), who owned the shield, is Darius, another of Alexander's opponents whose pursuit by Alexander around the East also features prominently in the romance. *Ector* (line 1106), the owner of the sword, is Hector, the Trojan war hero and son of Priam. Hector and Alexander were two of the Nine Worthies; Weiss, pp. 101–02, suggests that the equivalent description in *Gui de Warewic* was designed to portray Guy as a successor to the Nine Worthies and, thereby, to compare him implicitly with Arthur. This portrayal, however, has been somewhat weakened in the stanzaic *Guy* as only two of the Nine Worthies are represented. A third, Charlemagne, is included in *Gui de Warewic* (*rei Charles*, line 8390) but is replaced in the stanzaic *Guy* with *King Clarel*. The replacement may suggest an interest in representing warriors from the East or it may represent a particular knowledge of *Otuel* on the part of the redactor or scribe. For other examples of this type of heroic genealogy in romance, see *Floris and Blancheflour* (lines 177–84), in which the precious cup used to buy and then win back Blancheflour is linked to Aeneas and Caesar, and *Generydes*, in which the hero fights with a sword that once belonged to a prince "callid Julyan . . . sumtyme of Rome the Emperour" (lines 3400–01; ed. W. Aldis Wright, 2 vols., EETS o.s. 55, 70 [London: N. Trübner and Co., 1873–78]).

1112   *A targe listed with gold.* A light shield (usually small and round in shape); here described as either edged or banded with strips of gold.

1134   *Also brouke Y mi swere.* An oath: "As I may break my neck!" or, possibly, "Thus I keep my oath." See Whiting, N42 for an analogous example used as an emphatic: "As soon break his neck as his fast in that house."

1150   *With a river it ern al about.* Literally, the river "ran all around" the edge of the plain.

1171–82   The description of Amorant's sword answers the preceding description of Guy's weapons and armor (lines 1081–1119). The sword is said to have once been owned by the Greek hero Hercules but the identity of *Agnes* (line 1178) is uncertain. *Gui de Warewic* at this point states that "Une deuesse la li dona" (line 8467), that is, "a goddess" gave the sword to him. The auditory similarity suggests "Agnes" may have resulted from the Middle English scribe or redactor misunderstanding or mishearing "deuesse."

        The sword is said to have been imbued with special strength after having been *bathed in the flom of Helle* (line 1177), so that whoever wields it will be unbeatable. This reference associates Amorant with Achilles whose (near) infallibility was likewise achieved after he was dunked in the Styx. *The Seege or Batayle of Troy* records how Achilles' mother "bathid his body in þe flom of helle" (line 1345) and, with the exception of his feet which remained tender, his body turned "blak as Mahoun / Fro þe foot to þe croun / And his skyn was as hard as flynt" (line 1350–52). The process by which Achilles' skin achieved its flint-like hardness is subsequently reiterated in *The Seege* as a preface to the scene in which Achilles kills Hector in hand-to-hand combat (lines 1461–66). The association of Guy with Hector (he carries Hector's sword, line 1105) and Amorant with Achilles (his sword having the strength of Achilles) gives the battle another dimension. Portrayed as the descendants of these heroic ancestors, their meeting is dramatized in terms of the famous battle between Hector and Achilles, Trojan and Greek.

1201   *sadelbowe.* "The arched front part of a saddle, pommel" (*MED*).

1216–17   *"Lord," seyd Gii, "God Almight / That made the therkenes to the night."* This form of the rhetorical device "apostrophe" is very common in Anglo-Norman and Old French epics and their Middle English counterparts. Smithers (1988), p. 197, defines its use in these texts as involving "a reference to God or to Christ that specifies one or more of his attributes, or (more commonly) alludes to events in biblical history or in the life of Christ." It may be used in prayer, as a blessing, curse, oath, or greeting, in farewell, as a request, statement, or asseveration, in an interjection from the narrator, a confirmation of faith, or as hyperbole. The example here at lines 1216–17 conforms to a pattern which is repeatedly used in the stanzaic *Guy*, in which the first line has a call to God by name and the second refers to a biblical event. Comparable examples appear at lines 2353–54: "God

Almight / That winde and water and al thing dight"; and lines 2032–33: "'Lord,' seyd Gii, 'that with hond / Made wode, water, and lond.'" Dalrymple (2000), p. 128, observes that Guy consistently makes entreaties using this kind of pious expression (in which the omnipotent deity rather than the Passion is invoked) when he "seeks the protection and guardianship of God." For a discussion of pious expressions which invoke the Passion see the note to lines 257–58.

1230   *with his grimli gore. gore* < OE *gar* ("sword," "spear"). The line is formulaic; compare to *Amis and Amiloun*, "with his grimli gore"(line 1353); and *Horn Child and Maiden Rimnald*, "wiþ his grimli gare" (line 213); *Sir Isumbras*, "With grymly growndyne gare" (line 453).

1239   *stern and stive.* An alliterative formula for fierce, unbending severity. E.g., *William of Palerne*, "a stif man and a stern" (line 3378).

1255   *cercle of gold.* The metal band encircling the helmet.

1271   *hod.* A mail covering for the head and neck.

1275   *nasel.* The nose guard of a helmet.

1291–92   *nativité / Of Seyn Jon the martir fre.* Although the reference could be to John the Martyr, who, along with Paul the Martyr, was slain in the fourth century at Antioch, and is mentioned in Eucharistic prayers, the citation of the saint's nativity makes John the Baptist the more likely candidate. June 24 is the feast day celebrating his nativity, in which case the battle between Amourant and Guy would occur on June 23. The feast day of John the Martyr is June 26. Jacobus de Voragine gives some attention to John and Paul as among those who fell victim to Julian the Apostate, but the only detail given to link the two together is that they die as one for Christ. They do not appear in the *South English Legendary*. Although John the Baptist is not commonly referred to with the eponym "martyr," the fourteenth-century *Scottish Legend of the Saints* gives him three crowns, one for virginity, one for preaching, and one for martyrdom (*Legends of the Saints in the Scottish Dialect of the Fourteenth Century*, ed. W. M. Metcalfe, 3 vols., Scottish Text Society first ser. 13, 18, 23, 25, 35, 37 [Edinburgh: W. Blackwood and Sons, 1896; rpt. London: Johnson Reprint, 1968], 2.236, lines 461–72). He was an enormously popular saint with feast days both for his nativity (June 24) and his death by beheading (August 29). *The South English Legendary* combines events of both the nativity and martyrdom feasts, first celebrating his nativity ("the beste bern . . . that of womman was euere ibore withoute [except for] Iesu Crist" 1.244, line 2), but then concentrating on his martyrdom, with great emphasis on the ensuing miracles pertaining to his head and the finger that pointed out Christ that refused to burn when his headless body was cremated. That "in a castel of Arabie his heued was of ysmite" (1.243, line 45) perhaps lends a particular aptness to the beheading of Amorant in Arabie on the day before John the Baptist's nativity.

1296   *Of love was ther no speche.* This kind of ironic understatement, which uses litotes, is typical of the medieval epic style, especially in descriptions of battle. For further discussion of the influence of epic upon romance see Smithers (1988), p. 34, and David Burnley, "Comforting the Troops: An Epic Moment in Popular Romance," in Mills, Fellows, and Meale, pp.175–86.

1310   *so mot Y the.* "So may I thrive," "as I may prosper" (a common oath).

1322   *Now wald mi lord Ternagaunt.* According to the standard treatment of Islam in medieval romance and hagiography, "Ternavaunt" or "Sir Ternagaunt" (the most common form elsewhere is "Termagant") is regarded as one of the pagan gods worshipped by "Saracens." Saracens in romance also often swear by "Termagant" or by "Apolin," that is, "Apollo," as Colbrond does at line 3187. In *The Song of Roland*, the Saracens fight in the name of a trinity: Termagant, Apollo, and Muhammed.

1327–41   *For he hath destrud al our lawe . . . destrud our lay.* Amorant refers to an episode from Guy's youth in which he defended Constantinople from Saracen invasion (recounted in the couplet *Guy of Warwick*, lines 2869–4096). A similar reference is made by King Triamour at line 983. Guy's tendency to encounter figures from his former life develops the linked themes of penitence and identity. For another view of this aspect of the romance see Paul Price, "Confessions of a Godless Killer: *Guy of Warwick* and Comprehensive Entertainment" in *Medieval Insular Romance: Translation and Innovation*, ed. Judith Weiss, Jennifer Fellows, and Morgan Dickson (Cambridge, UK: D. S. Brewer, 2000), pp. 93–110.

1433   *drawe min hond.* Have strength or power to "turn my hand."

1567–69   *Bot at a strok as Amoraunt cast / Sir Gii mett with him in hast / And taught him a sori play.* The use of *cast* and *play* suggests punning upon the "casting" and "playing"' of dice, a game of chance.

Explanatory Notes

1716   *Me thenke thi paynes strong.* Perhaps originally "Me thenke thi payn es strong" (i.e., I think your pain is severe); compare to line 273.

1726–27   *For oft it falleth uncouthe man / That gode conseyle give can.* Whiting, M303, records this to be a common type of proverb in Middle English: "Uncouth (unknown) man oft can give good counseyl."

1762–63   *Now is his neve th'emperour steward, / His soster sone that hat Berard.* There are many examples in epic and romance of the privileged relationship between uncle and nephew. The significance of this relationship, especially between a man and his "sister's son," resides in the close and incontestable blood ties between these two men and the importance of their relationship for the stability of the dynasty. The relationship is not necessarily felicitous, but rather one of "schame" (line 1764), as was the fate of Mark and Tristram.

1810   *layd mi wedde.* Made a pledge "as a token and guarantee of intent to do battle" (*MED*).

1818   *borwe.* A legal term, "To become surety for [somebody] . . . guarantee the good behavior of, go bail for, to obtain the release of [somebody] . . . from prison or punishment" (*MED*).

1843–44   *No Sir Herhaud fond Y nought tare; / To seche Gyes sone he is fare.* Here reference is made to the existence of Reinbroun, the son who was conceived during the first days of Guy's marriage to Felice. Herhaud has gone in search of Reinbroun who, a subsequent reference reveals, has been stolen by travelling merchants: "To seche Gyes sone he is fare / That marchaunce hadde stollen thare" (lines 2836–37). The story of Reinbroun's capture and Herhaud's efforts to regain him constitutes a narrative off-shoot, of significant length and interest in its own right, that is explored in *Gui de Warewic* and in other Middle English redactions. In *Gui de Warewic*, the Reinbroun material is divided into two parts: the first, much shorter section appears midway through Guy's narrative (*Gui de Warewic* lines 8975–9392, intersecting the narrative during Guy's visit to Constantinople, which would be immediately after line 1692 in the stanzaic *Guy*); then, after Guy's death, the Reinbroun story is resumed and concluded (*Gui de Warewic*, lines 11657–12926, which would be after line 3576 in the *Stanzaic Guy of Warwick*). Although the redactor of the stanzaic *Guy* took care to omit this material, it was fashioned into a stanzaic romance in its own right by another East Midland redactor. The appearance of both romances together in the Auchinleck

143

MS suggests they may have been companion pieces and that production of the stanzaic *Guy* motivated the composition of *Reinbroun*.

1936–44   *Than seighe he an ermine com of his mouthe . . . / Anon Tirri gan wake.* This instance of an ermine creeping out of and back into a sleeping person's mouth is unique in romance. Marvelous and symbolic animals are, in general, a feature of romance, though dragons, horses, lions, dogs, and birds are the most common. See Bordman (1963).

1963–64   *And me thought Gii sat at min heved / And in his lappe me biweved.* In this context *lappe* has the meaning: "the lower part of a shirt, skirt, or habergeon; the front or back skirts of a divided garment" (*MED*).

1995   *Of charbukel the pomel.* The "pomel" refers to the knob at the end of the hilt of the sword. The name "carbuncle stone" was applied to precious stones of a red or fiery color, such as rubies, but also to a mythical gem said to emit light in the dark; see the note to lines 2986–88.

2084–85   *This seven winter no schaltow se / Noither fet no hond.* That is, his hands and feet would be severely bound. On *seven* as a sign of totality, see the note to line 3513, below.

2123   *wedde.* See note to line 1810.

2133   *Whereso thou may be sought.* A common verse phrase with diminished semantic force.

2168   *Prout and stern as a lipard.* That is, cunning and clever. The comparison is not necessarily derogatory and also appears in the romance *Richard Coer de Lyon*: "Than answered Kynge Rycharde, In dede lyon, in thought lybarde" (line 2194).

2224   *gerthes.* Saddle girths (the strap to secure each saddle).

2347–48   *The pilgrim waked and loked an heyghe, / The sterres on the heven he seighe.* Guy looks to the night stars for the second time in the romance. The decision to mark this the structural mid-point of the narrative (the interval during the second of three battles) with an echo of Guy's first contemplation of the stars seems entirely deliberate. Once again Guy's fate hangs in the balance, though this time his destiny is beyond his own control. This shift, from Guy being in control of his

144

own destiny to being "in God's hands," is a movement that is signalled at a number of other points in the narrative and is significant for the text's wider pious themes. The stars in this context, as Hopkins (p. 102) has pointed out, function as a "positive reminder of the greatness and glory of God" in contrast to the limited abilities of the individual human.

2352   *Bot winde and wateres wawe.* A metonymical expression to refer to the sea.

2353–70   The stanzaic *Guy* diverges from other versions in its presentation of Guy's prayer and subsequent rescue by the fisherman. Particularly significant is the addition of the emphatic statement (not found in the Anglo-Norman *Gui de Warewic* or the Caius MS 107 *Guy of Warwick*) that Christ himself saved Guy by sending the fisherman. In the Caius MS text, which offers a much closer rendering of the Anglo Norman, Guy's prayer focuses upon Berard's treachery and includes Guy cursing Berard:

> "God," he seyd, "all weldande,
> That stablyssheth both watre and londe,
> Lord, now thow thynke on mee;
> For I am betrayed now, I see.
> Lord, who hath do me thys ded?
> And I fyght for no mede,
> Ne for sylver ne for golde,
> But for my brother, my trowth to hold,
> And for to delyver hym owte of peryle,
> That longe hath bene in excile.
> Also power as he may bee.
> When I hym saw I had pyte:
> Sometyme he was a noble kny3t.
> I wold dye for Sir Terry is ryght.
> For he ys now so wrechyd a wyght,
> Ageyne Berrarde I toke the fyght.
> Yf I had the traytour slayne,
> Terry shuld have hys land ageyne.
> Lord, yf hyt my3t so be
> That he had helpe thorou3 me,
> And I wonne all hys land,
> And all the honoure to hys hand,
> Thow3 I levyd but till that daye,
> Hit were my joy, for soth I seye.
> But I am ded, well I wote:
> For me shall he never have state

145

Thorought treason of the Duke Barrard.
Have he never of hevyn parte!
He ys a thefe full of treason;
God geve hym hys malyson!"
Tho ther com a good fysshere
Fyshyng be Sir Gye nere.
The bed he saw far by fletand:
He turned hys bot and went nere hand. (lines 9776–9809)

2365   *striif.* This is the only instance of this sense of *striif* recorded by the *MED* (see "strife" n.2[d]).

2419   *Seyn Martin.* The emperor swears by St. Martin twice (also at line 2601). This is most likely to be Martin of Tours (c. 316–97). His legend was popular in the Middle Ages and is especially appropriate for the story of a pilgrim knight. Martin was a soldier who, after he dreamed of Christ as a beggar, became a beggar himself and then a monk. See Farmer, pp. 265–66.

2423   *dempt.* A legal term meaning "to declare guilty; to convict, condemn to death." See *MED*, *dampnen* n.2(a).

2431   *Therof give Y nought a chirston.* Whiting, C187, records this to be a common type of proverb in Middle English: "Not give a cherry-stone."

2500–04 *For bothe helmes he carf atuo . . . / Into the erthe wele half a fot.* Guy literally splits Berard in half from the top of his head down to the ground. The description is indebted to the similarly massive blows which feature in epic, such as the stroke dealt by Roland on Chernuble in *The Song of Roland*: "he breaks the helmet on which rubies gleam; he slices downward through the coif and hair and cuts between the eyes, down through his face, the shiny hauberk made of fine-linked mail, entirely through the torso to the groin, and through the saddle trimmed with beaten gold. The body of the horse slows down the sword, which, seeking out no joint, divides the spine: both fall down dead upon the field's thick grass" (lines 1326–34).

2592   *Thou do me londes lawe.* "To establish (sth.) by law, authorize, ordain." See *MED*, *lauen.*

2601   *Bi God and Seyn Martine.* See the note to line 2419.

146

2650–52   *Tho was sche founden in an ile / In a nunri that while / For doute of Berardes bond.* This episode can be compared to *King Horn* (lines 75–84): Horn's mother, in response to the pagan invasion and murder of her husband, goes to live alone "Under a roche of stone" (line 77) where she prays for her son and serves God in defiance of the pagan religion.

2683–2700   These episodes from Guy's earlier life are recounted in the couplet *Guy of Warwick*, though not quite in the order reported here. According to the alternative sequence, Guy helps Tirri in the following ways: (1) he finds Tirri lying grief stricken in a forest after having been assailed by outlaws (lines 4503–4690); (2) he rescues Tirri's beloved Oisel from the same outlaws (lines 4691–4734); (3) when Tirri is then carried off, he slays his captors (lines 4735–86); (4) he heals Tirri's wounds (lines 4819–4904); (5) he assists Tirri's father in battle (lines 4931–6094); (6) he delivers Tirri from Otoun's prison (lines 6095–6384); and (7) he slays Otoun and rescues Oisel just before they are married, then reunites Tirri and Oisel (lines 6385–6542).

2716–17   *He seyghe . . . yhosed ful wel.* Compare these lines to lines 1855–56.

2728–33   *Bot ich have a sone, ywis . . . in al thing.* Guy's response to Tirri's offer of a rich reward is to ask that the benefit of it be passed over to his son, Reinbroun. He later gives the same response to King Athelstan (lines 3304–06) when offered a reward for his services: "Ac yif Herhaud to this lond com / And bring with him Reynbroun mi sone / Help him Y thee biseche." Although Guy refuses these benefits for himself, Hopkins, p. 78, regards their deferral to his son as a sign that Guy "has not by any means abandoned worldly values in his striving for God" in the way that the model for his life, St. Alexis, does. Similarly, Dannenbaum, p. 359, highlights how Guy integrates a series of more worldly interests into his supposedly pious existence "in a way that, for Alexis, is out of the question."

2779–84   *And when the countas sikerly . . . laten him nought thennes gon.* Tirri's final humiliation is to be severely scolded by his wife. The way that Tirri is repeatedly rescued by Guy (see the note to lines 2683–2700) over the course of the legend has led Fewster, pp. 97–98, to propose that they represent two views of knighthood in symmetry. Tirri, she argues, "offers a set of alternatives to Guy's success," a "parallel but failing version of Guy himself," and "a backdrop of conflict and decline" against which Guy's idealized successes are played out.

2794   *At Winchester.* Winchester was a town of some importance between the tenth and twelfth centuries. Second in size after London, it shared the developing functions of a national capital. The association fostered with Guy of Warwick was apparently motivated by the popularity of the legend and an awareness of the prestige to be gained from a local connection. The account by Gerard of Cornwall (fl. 1350?) seems to have been particularly important in this respect. It presents a highly localized and selective version of the legend that focuses entirely on Guy's battle with Colbrond. Gerard names "Hyde Mede" near Winchester as the location for the battle and mentions that Colbrond's axe can still be seen in Winchester Cathedral (this axe is reported to have been held in the treasury of St. Swithun's Priory until the Dissolution). The rubric identifying Gerard states that his book was kept on a writing table close to the high altar of St. Stephen's Cathedral in Winchester. The account goes on to describe the hospice in Winchester, where Guy is alleged to have spent the night and which, it says, is located "250 paces in a northerly direction, where a new monastic building has now been built." Another association was suggested by Thomas Warton in the eighteenth century. He claimed to have seen a wall painting in the north transept of Winchester Cathedral when he was a boy which illustrated the fight between Guy and Colbrond. For a full discussion of these artifacts, see Richmond, pp. 70, 97–106.

2805   *Colbrond.* The *Sussex Lay Subsidy Rolls (1296–1332)* and the *Rolls of Knight's Fees in Kent (1254)* both record the surname "Colebrond," which is glossed as "firebrand" by the MED (*col*, n.2, 4[c]). The choice of this name, however, which can also be glossed "black sword," clearly has significance in terms of race and religious imagery; compare lines 2816, 3060, 3066, and 3079.

2836–37   See the note to lines 1843–44.

2923   *about prime.* Prime is the first canonical hour. That is, it is the monastic office or prayer service to be sung or recited at the first hour of the day, 6 a.m. (though the term can refer to the period between 6 and 9 a.m. when the next office begins). The sense here is "first thing in the morning."

2974   *To the king of Danmark he sent than.* In the manuscript each stanza is headed by a blue and red paraph sign with the exception of this stanza which has two paraphs. The second appears at this the tenth line and it may be intended to provide a visual marker to signal the beginning of Guy's final, climactic battle. See the facsimile editions by Pearsall and Cunningham and Burnley and Wiggins.

2984   *cercle.* See the note to line 1255, above.

2986–88   *In the frunt stode a charbukel ston / As bright as ani sonne it schon / That glemes under schawe.* Medieval lapidaries record the various virtues and special powers that precious stones were commonly believed to possess. This included the belief that certain stones shone with their own light, which would emanate even in dark places. References to such stones are not unusual in romance; for example, the magnificent cup in *Floris and Blancheflour* is surmounted by a carbuncle stone said to provide sufficient light for a butler to pour wine even in the darkest cellar (lines 171–75). For examples of Middle English lapidaries see: *A Middle English Lapidary*, ed. Arne Zettersten (Lund: Gleerups, 1968), and *English Mediaeval Lapidaries*, ed. Joan Evans and Mary S. Serjeantson, EETS o.s. 190 (London: Oxford University Press 1933; rpt. 1960).

2997   *targe listed.* See the note to line 1112.

2998–99   *Portreyd with thre kinges corn / That present God when He was born.* The offering of the Three Kings is an especially appropriate image for Guy to carry at this point in the text. As Dyas, p. 131, has observed, the journey of the Three Kings from the East to see the infant Christ "made them ideal role models for pilgrims." An image of kings, figures of the highest social rank, is also appropriate for Guy as the "king's champion." A similarly high-status appropriation of the image appears in the Chester Cycle of mystery plays where it was the wealthy and high-ranking guild of Mercers who presented the scene depicting the Three Kings' offerings. The *Pre-Reformation Chester Banns* makes special mention of the bright, shining, many-coloured fabrics used for the scene ("velvit, satten and damaske fyne / Taffyta sersnett of poppyngee grene," lines 69–71) and this great display of wealth indicates the Mercers' concern to associate themselves with an image that combined piety and prestige; see *The Banns of the Chester Plays*, ed. F. M. Salter (London: Oxford University Press, 1940).

3013–17   *rered Lazeroun . . . / And halp Daniel fram the lyoun.* The miracle in which Christ raised Lazarus from the dead appears in the New Testament (John 11), whereas Susanna and Daniel are both Old Testament figures: Susanna was rescued from the Jewish elders (Vulgate, Daniel 13) and Daniel was miraculously saved from the lions' den (Daniel 6:16–22). They are all examples of the kind of miraculous deliverance that Guy himself requires as he is about to enter a desperate situation. References to any of these biblical figures is rare in Middle English romance, though Dalrymple, pp. 133–35, records that prayers to Lazarus and Daniel appear

149

in *The Song of Roland* and the French *Romance of Horn*. A parallel also occurs in *Bevis of Hampton* at the moment when Bevis, finding himself in a similarly desperate situation to Guy, offers a prayer which refers to Lazarus: "Lord, that rerede the Lazaroun, / Dilivre me fro this fend dragoun!" (lines 2839–40).

3027–29   *After the relikes thai sende, / The corporas and the Messe gere. / On the halidom thai gun swere.* The "Messe gere" refers to the Eucharistic vestments and articles used for the swearing of oaths. These included the missal (the book containing the order of service for the Mass), the chalice (to hold the communion wine), the paten (to hold the host or bread wafer), and the corporal cloth or altar cloth on which all the Eucharistic elements were placed during consecration and with which they were subsequently covered. All of the "Messe gere" is sacred as it is essential to the re-enactment of Christ's death during the Mass, the principal Christian liturgical rite. The "halidom" can refer to either the sacred relics themselves or to a box containing sacred relics.

3061   *mailes*. The small metal rings or plates linked together in a mesh to make chain armor.

3064   *splentes of stiel*. Rod-like plates of steel.

3074   *bacinet*. "A hemispherical helmet, without a visor, worn under the fighting helmet" (*MED*).

3088   *gisarmes*. "A long-shafted battle ax or halberd with a knife-like point rising from the blade" (*MED*).

3094   *wicked hert*. Here "heart" refers to character or disposition. Compare, for example, to *Troilus and Criseyde* 3.736, where Pandarus calls Troilus a "wrecched mouses hert."

3115   *arsoun*. The pommel (the front of the saddle).

3137   *charbukel ston*. See the note to lines 2986–88.

3194–96   *Al sone he gan him turn tho . . . / Ther his axes stode bi hemselve*. This episode parallels Guy's request to Amorant for a drink of water (lines 1429–52 and 1513–24). In both cases, Guy appeals to his opponent's honor and sense of fair play, then, when he is denied, makes a dash for the item requested.

3236 *Te Deum laudamus thai gun sing.* The *Te Deum* is a hymn of praise (*Te Deum laudamus* being the opening words of this Latin hymn) sung during the night offices, especially matins, and on special occasions of thanksgiving. The "terminal" position of this hymn in the romance prompts Richmond to suggest that its choice "appropriately suggests that Guy's story is near conclusion" (Velma Bourgeois Richmond, *The Popularity of Middle English Romance* [Bowling Green, OH: Bowling Green University Popular Press, 1975], p. 186.)

3304–3306 See the note to lines 2728–33.

3340–48 *For thritten pouer men and yete mo / For hir lordes love sche loved so, / Ich day sche gan fede.* Woolgar, p. 154, records that "Alms from the table were a major element in charity associated with the great household." Felice is motivated to give alms regularly by the departure of her husband and, in this respect, can be compared to Josian, the heroine of *Bevis of Hampton*, who daily feeds and clothes poor pilgrims at the castle gates "For a knightes love, Bevoun" (line 2085). A contemporary parallel is offered by Joan de Valence, countess of Pembroke. Household accounts from September 1295 to September 1297 indicate that Joan regularly fed the poor and that after the death of her husband in May 1296 (when she took full responsibility for the household costs) the number of poor being fed increased from 8 to 21. See Woolgar, pp. 12–14, citing Public Record Office E101/505/25–7.

3361–72 *The levedi biheld him inliche . . . / Unto his lives ende.* The "wanderer returned" is an ancient theme, best known from Odysseus' return home to Penelope in Homer's *Odyssey*. Comparable episodes in medieval romance include *King Horn* lines 1089–1172 and *Bevis of Hampton* lines 2049–2235. Like Guy, Horn and Bevis each disguise themselves as a pilgrim and unrecognized receive alms from their beloved. However, whereas the disguise enables both Horn and Bevis to undertake a reconnaissance of a hostile locale, Guy enters his own home and faces no threat. Furthermore, whereas the identity of Horn and Bevis is dramatically revealed to the heroine, in the stanzaic *Guy* the episode pivots upon Guy's decision not to reveal his identity to Felice.

3367–69 *Of hire bere and of hir wine . . . / Oft sche gan him sende.* Robert Grosseteste's "Rules," a text from the first half of the thirteenth century which gives advice on dining, states that it was part of the role of the head of the household to ensure that food was distributed fairly and strangers were well provided for. In addition, the head of the household should ask for their dish to be piled high and passed around to offer extra portions to everyone. For further discussion of dining in the great household, see Woolgar, pp. 157–58.

3513   *A thousand angels and seven.* That there are a thousand "and seven" angels reflects the predilection in romance for conventional numbers of totality. For example, Guy is threatened with punishment for "seven winter" (line 2084); in *Bevis of Hamtoun*, Bevis lies in prison for "seven yare" (line 2001); and in *Havelok* the miraculous light shining from Havelok's mouth makes it seem as if "ther brenden serges sevene / And an hundred serges ok" (lines 2125–26). Other conventional numbers have religious or symbolic resonances. Thus Guy fights three battles and Felice feeds "thritten" poor men each day (lines 3340 and 3354).

3524–27 *A swete brathe com fram his bodi / That last that day so long / That in this world spices alle / No might cast a swetter smalle.* The smell of spices was regarded as a miraculous sign indicating a holy presence. Christ and the Virgin are regularly described in epithets as sweet spices (see 2 Corinthians 2:14–16): in *Ecce ancilla* (in *Religious Lyrics of the Fifteenth Century*, ed. Carleton Brown [London: Oxford University Press, 1939], pp. 105–06) the Virgin is hailed and told she shall "conceyve a swete spyce" (line 5) and, in *Heil be þou marie þe* (in *Hymns to the Virgin and Christ*, ed. Frederick J. Furnivall, EETS o.s. 24 [London: N. Trübner and Co., 1868; rpt. New York: Greenwod Press, 1969], pp. 4–5), she is addressed as "spice swettist of savour" (line 29). Marvels, magic, and wonders feature regularly in medieval romance but the application of a posthumous miracle of this kind to a romance protagonist is remarkable and shows the extent of hagiographical influence upon the text. In only one other romance, *Sir Gowther*, do posthumous miracles of this kind occur to the protagonist. After death, Sir Gowther is described as a true saint (a "varré corsent parfett," line 727) for whose faithfulness God performs miracles: he "garus tho blynd to see / And tho dompe to speyke," he "makus tho crokyd ryght. / And gyffus to tho mad hor wytte / Any mony odur meracullus" (lines 739–43).

Textual Notes

100	*fayn*. MS: *faym*.
107	*lord*. MS: *lod*.
180	*gret*. MS: *gre*.
601	*sone*. MS: *som*, with the *o* altered from *n*.
664	*cleped*. MS: *clepd*.
675	*were*. MS: second *e* added above the line.
800	*ther no man*. MS: *þer man*.
853	*trewthe yplight*. MS: *trewþe y*, with *pliȝt* inserted above the line.
855	*he*. MS: *ich*.
863	*swich sorwe, ywis*. MS: *swiche ywis sorwe*, with *sorwe* added to the margin by a later hand.
900	*preved*. MS: *proued*.
1018	*mi*. MS: *m* altered from *y*.
1029	A line has been erased after this line in the MS.
1031	*help*. MS: *hep*.
1034	*to.* MS: preceded by an erased *þe*.
1044	*warld*. MS: *wald*.
1069–71	These lines are included in the previous stanza in the MS.
1080	*Bateyle for*. MS: *Batelye of him for*, with *of him* canceled.
1091	*thai thought*. MS: *þai it þouȝt*.
1204	*wem*. MS: *when*.
1227	*sore*. MS: *o* altered from *a*.
1272	*the*. MS: *þe þe*.
1336	*and*. MS: *7* inserted above the line.
1362	*lond*. MS: *lond lond*, with cancellation marks under the second.
1373	*ful glad sikerli*. MS: *ful glad ful sikerli*, with second *ful* crossed out.
1410	*fleye*. Altered from *fleyee* in the MS.
1440	*For Godes love*. MS: *for love*. Emended for sense and meter.
1441	*seyd*. MS: preceded by an erased *þ*.
1447	*Gii*. Marked for insertion at the end of the line in MS.
1547	*thou*. MS: *þo*.
1582	*was faynting*. MS: *was gin faynting*.
1603	*was*. Inserted below the line in the MS.

1627	*thou*. Inserted above the line in the MS with correct position marked.
1741	*wrong*. Inserted above *gret* in the MS.
1782	*is*. Altered from *it* in the MS.
1784	*pouer of*. MS: *pouer for of*, with *for* canceled.
1791	*out*. MS preceded by canceled *his lond*.
1797	*sent*. MS: preceded by canceled *u* or *n*.
1798	*Y*. Altered from *Þ* in the MS and followed by a canceled *ai*.
1802	*with wicked pourt*. MS: *þe wicked pourt*. *MED* supports the preposition *yn* for this construction (see *port* n.4 [1a]), but *with* makes more sense in this particular context.
1808	*Otoun*. MS: *of toun*.
1822	*Berard*. MS: *Bernard*, with cancellation mark under the *n*.
1836	*Otoun*. MS: *of toun*.
1849	The rubricated paraph that originally appeared at the head of this stanza has been erased and replaced with a rubricated initial *S*. This initial was painted by a different limner than the others in the text and is cruder in style.
1877	*hende*. MS: altered from *hente*.
1888	*treuthe*. MS: *treþe*, with *u* inserted above and its correct position marked.
1893	*ded*. MS: altered from *dede*.
1952	*thin eighe*. MS: *þi neiʒe*.
1953	*y*. MS: *þou*.
1965	*dest*. MS: *dost*.
1970	*sweven*. MS: *seuen*.
1979	*tresour*. MS: *resour*.
1987	*Gii*. MS: inserted above the line with correct position marked.
1996	*it*. MS: superscript.
2002–04	Missing in MS.
2042	*Gii*. MS: inserted above the line with correct position marked.
2047	*seyd*. MS: inserted above the line with correct position marked.
2113	*Berrard*. MS: *Berrad*. See also line 2149.
2119	*Gii*. MS: inserted above the line with correct position marked.
2149	*Berrard*. MS: *Berrad*. So, too, line 2113.
2197	*stount*. MS: *ston*.
2240	*Beter*. MS: *Berter*.
2245	*Strong*. MS: *Srong*.
2263	*herd telle that the pilgrim*. MS: *herd telle pilgrim*.
2280	Missing in MS.
2326–27	An inkblot obscures the beginning of these two lines in the MS.
2390	*with*. MS: *þ* inserted above the line.

2402	*at.* MS: *atte*, with cancellation marks under *te*.
2414	*swore.* MS: *s* inserted above the line.
2423	*dempt.* MS: *demp*.
2485	There is no paraph sign to indicate the opening of this stanza in the MS.
2488	*him.* MS: omitted but included in the catchword (at the foot of fol.160vb): *he hit him on þe helm.*
2506–08	An inkblot obscures the initial letters of these three lines in the MS.
2549	*wraied.* MS: *wraid*.
2592	*Thou.* MS: *Þo*.
2607	*there.* MS: *þre*.
2615	*thin em.* MS: *þi nem*.
2803	*hem.* MS: *him*.
2814	*toun.* MS: altered from *doun*.
2822	*Inglond.* MS: *Inglong*.
2833	*is Herhaud.* MS: *iherhaud*.
2867	*and.* MS: *7 7*.
2878	*Stil.* MS: *Til*.
2951	*þe.* Inserted above the line in the MS.
2968	*God.* MS: followed by a second, erased *god*.
2984	*cercle.* MS: *cecle*.
2991	*bihold.* MS: *bhold*.
3031	*ywis.* MS: inserted above *furst* to maintain column width.
3068	*splentes.* MS: *spentes*.
3088	*Axes.* MS: *Axs*.
3095	*aferd.* MS: *d* altered from *t*.
3199	*Colbrond.* MS: *Colbron*.
3208	*dint.* MS: preceded by erased *de*.
3213	*wounde.* MS: *o* altered from *a*.
3222	*gan.* MS: omitted.
3280	*mi.* MS: *þi mi*.
3299	*Half.* MS: *In half*.
3301	*Gii.* MS: added above (possibly in a later hand).
3364	*dring.* MS: *ding*.
3373	*Gii.* MS: omitted.
3503	*sche.* MS: *ssche*, with the initial *s* marked for deletion.
3529	*levedy.* MS: *leudy*.
3559	*say.* MS: *day*.
3587	*that.* MS: *þai*.

Index of Place Names

Place names from the text are given in bold and followed by their current geographical equivalent (as far as this is possible). Additional information indicates the location of regions and cities and the historical significance of certain names. For further information and historical maps of the region, see Colin McEvedy, *The Penguin Atlas of Medieval History* (Harmondsworth, UK: Penguin, 1961).

Alisaundre, Alisaunder (616, 640, 932, 1606) Alexandria (city, Egypt).

Almayn(e), Almaine (831, 1699) Germany.

Antiage (530) Antioch (city, Turkey).

Aquitayne (837) Aquitaine (region, S.W. France).

Ardern (803) The ancient forest of Arden was located in northwest Warwickshire and Henley-in-Ardern was a major market town in this region.

Aufrike (2816) Africa.

Bars (835) This reference was added by the Middle English redactor. It may be a shortened version of "Barbary" which in Middle English could either refer generally to Muslim ("Saracen") lands or, more specifically, to the Islamic north coast of Africa (Morocco, Algeria, Tunisia). If this is the case, it is an unusual variant form (with no other examples recorded in the *MED*), devised in order to rhyme with "Tars." An alternative, though less likely, possibility is that "Bars" refers to the historical region of that name in Slovakia.

Bedlem (524) Bethlehem.

Borgoine (839) Burgundy (region, C. France).

Braban (835) Brabant (an independent province in what is now the Netherlands and Belgium).

Breteyne (500, 840) Brittany (region, N.W. France).

Calaber (830) Calabria (region, S. Italy).

Cisil (838) Sicily.

Costentin, Costentyn (1335, 1692, 1693, 2051, etc.) Constantinople, now Istanbul (city, N.W. Turkey).

Coyne, lond of (829) Konya (the ancient city of Iconium). Located in Turkey (in the area of Lycaonia), it was the capital of the sultans of the Seljuk Turks from 1063 to 1309 and remains one of the holy cities of Islam.

Cristianté (489) Christian lands.

Danmark(e) (2809, 2857, 2938, 2974, etc.) Denmark.

Durras, th'erldam of (579, 1661, 1681) Durrës (city, W. Albania).

Espire, that riche cité (1076, 1702) Spires (city on the Rhine, S.W. Germany), capital of the Bavarian palatinate. At line 1702, "Espire" specifies the location of Guy and Tirri in Germany. However, the reference to "Espire" at line 1076 seems to be either a scribal error or an oversight on the part of the Middle English redactor as it refers to the location of the Sultan's court in the East. At this point the Anglo-Norman *Gui de Warewic* locates the Sultan's court within "Perse" (line 8384), that is, "Persia."

Fraunce (500, 833, 1170) France.

Gastoine (839) Gascony (region, S.W. France).
Gormoys (1756) Worms (city, S.W. Germany), capital of the Holy Roman Emperor.
Grece (1109, 1687) Greece.
Grekis See (486, 2049) the eastern Mediterranean Sea.

Hethenisse (1346) non-Christian lands or Muslim lands.
Humber (472) the Humber (river, N. England).
Hungri (838) Hungary.

Inglond (19, 429, 508, 841, etc.) England.

Jerusalem (523, 593, 1086, 1633, etc.) Jerusalem.

Kent (473) Kent (county, S. E. England).

Lombardy(e) (502, 832, 2432) Lombardy (region, N. Italy).
Londen (471) London (city, England).
Loreyn, Lorain (467, 502, 3572) Lorraine (region, N. E. France).
Louthe (471) Louth (town, Lincolnshire).

Normondye (499, 833) Normandy (region, N. France)
Northhumberlond (23) Northumberland (county, England).

Pavi (1759, 1892, 2138, 2201, etc.) Pavia (town, Lombardy).
Perci (2051) Persia.
Poil (835) Apulia (region, S. E. Italy).
Portesmouthe (474) Portsmouth (town, S. England).

Ragoun (838) Ragusa, now Dubrovnik (city, Croatia).
Romayne (839) Romania, meaning Byzantium. See McEvedy (1961), p. 30n1: "the 'Byzantines' never used the term in this way themselves; right to the end they called themselves and their empire Roman. Westerners agreed about the empire ('Romania') but referred to its inhabitants as Greeks. The Greeks called all westerners Franks."

Glossary of Common Hard Words and Middle English Romance Idioms

This glossary supplements the glosses within the text and includes (1) difficult words that are common and therefore not glossed in the text on every occurrence; (2) idiomatic forms characteristic of ME romance for which there is not sufficient space in the text to give a full definition.

ac (adv., prep., conj.) *but*

also (conj.) *as; in addition*

amorwe, at morwe (adv.) *in the morning, on the following morning*

-and(e) (present participle suffix) *-ing*

anonright (adv.) *soon, immediately*

anour (n.) *honor*

aplight (adv.) *in faith, forsooth;* used emphatically, usually in rhyme and with diminished force.

ar(e) ⟶ **er**

asayl(e), aseyl(e) (v.) *attack, assault*

astow (elision) *as you*

axen (ax(e), axi, axed, axse) (v.) *ask*

ayn ⟶ **eighe(n)**

bad (p.t.) *asked, begged; prayed, said a prayer*

bale (n.) *pain, misery, suffering*

barfot (adv.) *barefoot*

barnage (n.) *the body of nobles or retainers of a ruler or king, the nobility*

baroun (n.) *a member of the nobility, ranking below an earl and above a knight; a hero, warrior, any man of honor; master of a household*

bede (n.) *prayer; request, command*

beld ⟶ **bold**

bern(e) (n.) *person, man*

best (adj.) *finest, highest in rank*

bi (prep.) *beside, along, through means of, at, in, on;* (adv.) ~ **(God, etc.)**, *as surely as one believes in;* (n.) *town;* (v.) *be*

biforn (adv.) *before him/her(self), in front of him/her(self); in advance of; at a previous time*

biteche (v.) *grant, entrust, commend, leave;* often used in salutation on taking leave: *God be with you! Goodbye!*

ble (n.) *face, skin color, complexion*

blithe (adj.) *joyful, happy, gracious; beautiful*

bold, beld (adj.) *brave, courageous, powerful, mighty, excellent, noble, fair*

bot (conj.) *apart from, unless, merely, only, however, moreover;* (n.) *boat;* (pp.) *cut*

bounde (p.t.) *dominated, overcame (by love, suffering, pain);* (adj.) *strong*

161

Glossary

boundé, bounté (n.) *goodness, virtue, knightly prowess, strength, kindness, mercy, generosity, liberality*

bour (n.) *lady's chamber or quarters, inner suite or room*

bright (adj.) *having a fresh, rosy complexion; beautiful, shining (with health); sunny; of armor or weapons: untarnished, gleaming*

brond (n.) *sword, blade*

broun (adj.) *of steel, weapons etc.: shining, polished, bright*

care (n.) *sorrow, distress, concern*

carf (pp.) *carved*

certes (adv.) *certainly, of course*

chere (n.) *facial expression, mien, state of mind, mood; appearance*

cleped (p.t.) *called*

clere (adj.) *shining, gleaming, glittering, magnificent, excellent*

curteys (adj.) *refined in manners, courtly, benevolent, generous, respectful, meek*

dede (p.t.) *did*

del (n.) *part, portion, bit*

dent(es) ⇒ **dint(es)**

dight (ydight) (v.) *prepare, prepared; dress, dressed, armed; condemn; made, did*

dint(es), dent(es) (n.) *blow(s)*

diol (n.) *sorrow*

diolful (adj.) *sorrowful, distressing*

douhti (adj.) *brave, fierce, excellent, honorable, handsome*

doun (n.) *hill*

drede (n.) *fear, anxiety, unease, danger;* (v.) *fear*

dreri, drery (adj.) *sorrowful, dejected, apprehensive*

egre (adj.) *eager; fierce in battle; angry, spirited;* ~ **of mode** *angrily, impetuously*

eighe(n), eyghen, ayn (n.) *eye(s)*

eke (adv., conj.) *also*

elders (n.) *ancestors*

em(e) (n.) *uncle*

er, ar(e), or (adv., conj., prep.) *before*

everilcan, everilkan (pron., elision) *every one, every single one*

everich (pron., elision) *every each,* with the sense: *each one, any one*

everichon (pron., elision) *every each one, every single one*

evermo, evermore (adv.) *evermore, constantly*

eyghen ⇒ **eighe(n)**

faile, fayle (n.) **withouten ani** ~ *without doubt, surely, truly*

fain ⇒ **fayn**

fair (adj.) *beautiful; noble, gentle; courteous; splendid, excellent;* of weather: *clear, bright*

fale, fele (adj., indefinite number) *many, much*

fare (v.) *go,* or *gone; proceed;* (n.) *behavior, demeanor; course, track*

fawe ⇒ **fayn**

fayn, fain, fawe (adj.) *joyful, eager;* (adv.) *willingly, eagerly*

fe (n.) *wealth, property;* also, *land held on condition of service to a feudal lord*

feffen (feffed, feffe) (v.) *to endow, furnish with a gift; to put (an estate in land) in a person's possession*

Glossary

fel (adj.) *shrewd, clever; fierce in combat; stern; wrathful, brutal;* (v.) *fell; befell; to bring to ground*

fele ➺ **fale**

fere (n.) *companion, fellow soldier, friend;* (adv.) **y ~, in ~** *together, in company together* or *at the same time;* (adj.) *complete*

floures (n.) *flowers;* often denoting ornamental decoration on a helmet

fond (p.t.) *met with, discovered, found;* (v.) *to attempt, undertake; to test; seek;* **up ~** *to thrust up*

fong (v.) *undertake*

forgon (p.t.) *lost*

forlorn, forlore, lorn (p.t.) *lost, abandoned*

forward (adv.) *henceforth, hereafter;* (n.) *agreement, pact*

fot-hot (adv.) *quickly, immediately*

foule (adj.) *ugly, hideous; evil, wicked; shameful*

frain, frein (v.) *ask, inquire*

fre (adj.) *having the social statue of a noble or a freeman; noble, generous, gracious*

frein ➺ **frain**

fro (conj.) *from*

ful (adv.) used as an intensifier: *very, extremely*

gambisoun (n.) *a quilted jacket or tunic worn under armor*

game(n) (n.) *amusement(s), pleasure*

gan ➺ **ginnen**

gentil (adj.) *of noble rank or birth; having the manners prescribed by the ideals of chivalry: nobility, kindness, courtesy*

gest (n.) *poem, song, tale, chivalric romance*

ginnen (gan, gun, gon) (v.) *begin.* Often used as an auxiliary relating to actions, motions or events; in these cases it is almost without meaning but can be rendered as *do, did.*

glad (adj.) *joyful; gracious; delighted*

glaive (n.) *a lance or spear,* possibly also some kind of sword or falchion

gle (n.) *merrymaking, entertainment, pleasure*

glotoun (n.) *a glutton; a villain, wretch*

gome (n.) *man; warrior*

gon ➺ **ginnen**

grame (v.) *infuriate, anger;* (n.) *hatred, rage*

gramerci (interjection) *thanks, many thanks*

greven (agreved, greveth, greved) (v.) *enrage; to cause sorrow; to cause physical pain*

grille (adj.) *angry, fierce; horrible; strong*

grim (adj.) *fierce, cruel; hideous, monstrous, ugly, overgrown*

grimli, grimly (adj.) *fierce, cruel, angry; terrifying, hideous; dangerous, deadly;* of wounds, pains: *severe*

griseli, grisely, griselich (adj.) *horrible, ugly*

gun ➺ **ginnen**

halvendel (n.) *half portion of something, half*

halwen (n.) *shrines (of saints), holy places*

hardi (adj.) *bold, courageous*

hastow (elision) *have you*

hauberjoun (n.) *coat or jacket of mail*

he (pron.) *he; in rhyme, they*

hem (pron.) *them; themselves, each other*

hende, hendi, hendy (adj.) *noble, having courtly or knightly qualities; near, close by*

hent (v.) *seize, grasp*

her (pron.) *their*

hete (n.) *hatred, anger; thirst; haste*

heved (n.) *head*

heye, heighe, heyghe (n.) **(on, an, in)** ~ *at once, immediately, quickly; above*

hight ⇒ **hoten**

him (pron.) *him; himself*

hond (n.) *hand; hands;* **(take, nim) on** ~ *undertake;* **in(to) (his, min etc)** ~**, on** ~**, an** ~ *into (someone's) possession, in(to) (someone's) hand;* **bi (the)** ~ *by the hand;* **an** ~**, on** ~ *assuredly, certainly;* **douhti(nes) of (thin)** ~ *martial skill or bravery*

hondes, honden (n.) *hands*

honour (n.) *rank; worldly glory, fame; nobleness, virtue*

hose, hos(s)en (n.) *leg wear; armor for the lower legs, leg guards*

hoten, hight (p.t.) *called, named*

hye (pron.) *she*

ich (pron.) *I; each, every; same*

icham *I am*

ichave *I have*

ichem *I them*

ichil *I shall, I will*

ichim *I him*

ichon *each one*

is (pron.) *his*

ivel (adj.) *painful; ill; wicked;*

unfortunate; (adv.) *poorly, inadequately;* (n.) *misfortune, trouble*

iwis, ywis (adv.) *certainly, for sure, indeed, truly;* a common romance tag often used in rhyme

kende (adj.) *noble; constant, faithful; brave; loving, affectionate*

kene (adj.) *brave; fierce; shrewd, sharp*

kerveand, kerveinde (present participle as adj.) *sharp edged, sharp pointed*

kithe (v.) *know*

knawe ⇒ **knowen**

kne(s) (n.) *knee(s)*

knowen (knowe, knawe, knawen) (v.) *to recognize, identify; know*

lef ⇒ **leve**

leman (n.) *loved one, paramour, wife;* often used as a term of intimate address: *sweetheart, darling*

lesing (v.) *lying*

leve, lef (adj.) of a person: *beloved, dear, esteemed;* (n.) *permission, leave;* (v.) *believe; remain, stay; permit, enable*

levedi (n.) *lady*

lever (adv.) *rather, prefer*

-lich(e) (adverbial suffix) *-ly*

lorn ⇒ **forlorn**

Mahoun (proper n.) *Muhammad*

maistri (n.) *victory, dominance*

me (pron.) *me; myself*

mede (n.) *reward*

melody, melodi (n.) *social harmony; vocal or instrumental harmony*

merci (n.) *pardon; compassion, kindness, friendship;* as an exclamation: *Have mercy! Spare me!* or *Thanks!*

mete (n.) *food, a meal*

miche, michel (adj.) *large; much, great; many*

mighten (v.) *to be able to; should, would*

morwe ⟶ **amorwe**

mounde (n.) *power, strength; excellence, value, nobility*

nam ⟶ **nimen**

nar *are not*

nas *was not*

nere *were not*

nil *will not*

niltow *will you not*

nimen (nam, nim, nom, nomen) (v.) *to take; to enter*

nis *is not*

nist *knew not*

nold *would not*

not *know not*

nought (n.) *nothing; not*

o (prep.) *on, of, in, to;* (num.) *one;* (int.) as an exclamation: *oh!*

of (prep.) *of; off*

olive (adj.) *alive*

or ⟶ **er**

ostel (n.) *lodgings, accommodation;* (v.) *to lodge, receive accommodation*

ous (pron.) *us*

page (n.) *lowest-ranking servant in a royal, noble or ecclesiastical household; a personal servant or attendant*

par charité *as an act of kindness, for the sake of charity;* often used as an intensifier or in entreaties and requests

parlement (n.) *a hearing before gathered representatives where judgement may be passed and laws enacted*

plate (n.) *plate armor*

plight (v.) *promise, pledge,* often in the tag "I plight," *I assure you, I swear; pulled, pulled out*

pouer (adj.) *poor*

pride (n.) *glory, honor, good repute; ostentation, splendor, opulence; ferocity, arrogance*

priis, pris (n.) *reward, prize;* often with reference to the reward for the winner of the chivalric tournament or martial games; *fame, renown; event; wealth; victory;* **of** ~ *excellent;* **for** ~ *as the most excellent; praise*

proude, prout (adj.) *proud;* compare to **pride**

quite (v.) *pay, give reward;* ~ **and skere** of a person, *blameless, proved innocent;* ~ **and clene** *completely*

quite-claim, quite-claym, quite-cleymed (v.) *to be released without any hindrance and with any legal claims relinquished (that is, with property and possessions returned)*

rede (v.) *advise, counsel; read; interpret;* (n.) *advice, plan*

reweful (adj.) *pitiful, painful*

rewthe (n.) *pity*

right (adv.) often used as an intensifier, *indeed, directly, exactly, very, properly*; also in various combinations with the sense *directly, at once:* **ful** ~; **forth** ~; **anon** ~; **now** ~; (n.) *justice, correct law;* **with**~ *rightly, in accordance with the moral code;* (adj.) *correct, proper;* as opposed to left.

Rode (n.) *Cross*

sale (n.) *the main hall of a palace, castle or mansion*

sare ⇒ **sore**

saunfaile, saunfayl(e) (adv.) *without doubt, surely, truly*

schaltow *shall you*

schende ⇒ **schent**

schene (adj.) *beautiful; bright, luminous*

schent, schende (p.t.) *destroyed, ruined, condemned*

schrive (v.) *to administer the sacrament of penance, to hear someone's confession, to absolve someone*

schop(e) (p.t.) *shaped, created*

sclavain, sclavayn (n.) *a cloak,* in particular here: *a pilgrim's cloak or mantle*

selve (adj.) *same*

servise (n.) *Christian worship, especially the Mass*

sesen (sese, sesed) (v.) *to endow or enfeoff something, to put a kingdom, land, estate in legal or formal possession*

sethe, sethen ⇒ **sithe**

seye ⇒ **seyghe**

seyghe, seighe, seye (v.) *saw*

siken (sikeing, siked) (v.) *to sigh*

sikerly, sikerliche (adv.) *certainly, for sure*

singen (sing) (v.) *to say, repeat, cry, sing*

sithe, sithen, sethe, sethen (n.) *times;* (adv.) *then, since, after, afterwards*

smiten (smite, smot) (v.) *to strike, blow; to pierce, penetrate; to afflict, kill; sever*

socour (n.) *(military) assistance, help, champion*

socourd (p.t.) *assisted, saved*

sond (n.) *the grace or ordinance of God; a summons, command; a messenger; land, ground*

song (n.) *speech, words, cry*

sore, sare (adj.) *painful; grievous, bitter, miserable; intense, hard to endure*

sorwe (n.) *grief, sadness; misfortune; physical pain*

sothe (n.) *truth;* ~ **to say** *in truth, to tell the truth;* used emphatically in rhyme.

soudan (n.) *the sultan,* a Muslim ruler.

spouse (spousy, spoused) (v.) *marry, married*

stede (n.) *place; horse*

stern (adj.) *harsh; brave; alarming, frightening*

stille (adj.) *silent, quiet; motionless;* (adv.) *meekly, patiently; continually;* **bileft** ~ *remained in that same state;* (v.) *to stop, cease*

stirt (p.t.) *jumped;* ~ **up, up** ~, *leaped up*

stithe (adj.) *strong, hardy*

stive (adj.) *strong, sturdy*

stounde, stonde (n.) *moment, particular time or length of time*

stout (adj.) *bold, fierce, skilled in battle; noble; strong, sturdy;* (adj.) *powerful, having strength, severe*

swithe (adv.) *quickly, swiftly;* **as~, also~, als~** *at once, immediately; very, extremely*

than (v.) *then*

that (conj.) *so that, in order that, with the result that; and*

thee (pron.) *you; your, yours; yourself; this*

thei (conj.) *though*

th'emperour (n.) *the emperor*

ther (adv.) *there; where*

th'erl (n.) *the earl*

thewes (n.) *courtly conduct, noble customs, qualities and principles*

tho (adv.) *then; when;* (pron.) *those*

thou (pron.) *you*

thriddendel (n.) *one third part*

thritten (num.) *thirteen*

tide, tyde (n.) *time*

tite (adv.) **as~, als~** *immediately, right away, as soon as possible*

to (prep.) *to;* (num.) *two*

to- (verbal prefix) *utterly, to pieces*

todrawe (v.) *pull apart by horses, dismember, disembowel*

tour (n.) *tower*

treuthe (n.) *pledge, promise, loyalty*

tuo (num.) *two*

tyde ⇒ **tide**

uncouthe (adj.) *alien, foreign, strange*

unrede (adj.) *excessive, huge, monstrous*

unride (adj.) *violent, unrestrained*

unsemli, unsemly (adj.) *ugly, barbarous*

ventayle (n.) *a piece of chain mail to protect the lower face, neck, and upper chest*

verrament, varray (adv.) *to be sure, certainly, indeed, truthfully;* a common metrical tag used here in rhyme with diminished emphatic force

verray ⇒ **verrament**

wald (v.) *would, wish, be willing to;* frequently used as a model auxiliary expressing intention, purpose or a desire or willingness to do something

way (n.) *road, path; journey,* or specifically *pilgrimage*

wede (n.) *clothing, attire*

wel(e) (adv.) used as an intensifier, *very, much, extremely; appropriately, properly;* with amounts, *at least, no less than; elegantly;* (v.) *will*

wenden (wende, wendeth) (v.) *to walk, travel, wander; to return; to believe, hope*

whilom (adv.) *once, at one time, formerly*

wight (n.) *person, creature, man, woman; a small quantity, bit;* (adj.) *brave, valiant*

wiltow *will you*

wise (adj.) *prudent, discerning; knowledgeable*

wist: ⇒ **witen**

wit (n.) *mind*

witen (wist, wite, wost, wot) (v.) *to know; to believe, expect*

wive (n.) *wife; woman*

wo (n.) *misery; misfortune;* (adj.) *wretched, distressed*

wode (adv.) *mad, crazed, berserk*
wond (v.) *to hold back, hesitate;* (p.t.) *went*, ➻ **wenden**
wost ➻ **witen**
wot ➻ **witen**
wrong (n.) *wickedness, injustice; harm, physical damage; sorrow;* (p.t.) *wrung*

y- past participle prefix
yare, yore (adv.) *quickly, eagerly; prepared, ready*
yede (p.t.) *went*
yepe (adj.) *clever, skilled; agile, eager*
yere (n.) *year*
yif, yive (conj.) *if*
yore ➻ **yare**
ywis ➻ **iwis**

Volumes in the Middle English Texts Series

The Floure and the Leafe, *The Assembly of Ladies*, and *The Isle of Ladies*, ed. Derek Pearsall (1990)

Three Middle English Charlemagne Romances, ed. Alan Lupack (1990)

Six Ecclesiastical Satires, ed. James M. Dean (1991)

Heroic Women from the Old Testament in Middle English Verse, ed. Russell A. Peck (1991)

The Canterbury Tales: Fifteenth-Century Continuations and Additions, ed. John M. Bowers (1992)

Gavin Douglas, *The Palis of Honoure*, ed. David Parkinson (1992)

Wynnere and Wastoure and The Parlement of the Thre Ages, ed. Warren Ginsberg (1992)

The Shewings of Julian of Norwich, ed. Georgia Ronan Crampton (1993)

King Arthur's Death: The Middle English Stanzaic Morte Arthur and Alliterative Morte Arthure, ed. Larry D. Benson and Edward E. Foster (1994)

Lancelot of the Laik and Sir Tristrem, ed. Alan Lupack (1994)

Sir Gawain: Eleven Romances and Tales, ed. Thomas Hahn (1995)

The Middle English Breton Lays, ed. Anne Laskaya and Eve Salisbury (1995)

Sir Perceval of Galles and Ywain and Gawain, ed. Mary Flowers Braswell (1995)

Four Middle English Romances: Sir Isumbras, Octavian, Sir Eglamour of Artois, Sir Tryamour, ed. Harriet Hudson (1996)

The Poems of Laurence Minot (1333–1352), ed. Richard H. Osberg (1996)

Medieval English Political Writings, ed. James M. Dean (1996)

The Book of Margery Kempe, ed. Lynn Staley (1996)

Amis and Amiloun, Robert of Cisyle, and Sir Amadace, ed. Edward E. Foster (1997)

The Cloud of Unknowing, ed. Patrick J. Gallacher (1997)

Robin Hood and Other Outlaw Tales, ed. Stephen Knight and Thomas Ohlgren (1997)

The Poems of Robert Henryson, ed. Robert L. Kindrick (1997)

Moral Love Songs and Laments, ed. Susanna Greer Fein (1998)

John Lydgate, *Troy Book: Selections*, ed. Robert R. Edwards (1998)

Thomas Usk, *The Testament of Love*, ed. R. Allen Shoaf (1998)

Prose Merlin, ed. John Conlee (1998)

Middle English Marian Lyrics, ed. Karen Saupe (1998)

John Metham, *Amoryus and Cleopes*, ed. Stephen F. Page (1999)

Four Romances of England: King Horn, Havelok the Dane, Bevis of Hampton, Athelston, ed. Ronald B. Herzman, Graham Drake, and Eve Salisbury (1999)

The Assembly of Gods: Le Assemble de Dyeus, or Banquet of Gods and Goddesses, with the Discourse of Reason and Sensuality, ed. Jane Chance (1999)

Thomas Hoccleve, *The Regiment of Princes*, ed. Charles R. Blyth (1999)

John Capgrave, *The Life of St. Katherine*, ed. Karen Winstead (1999)

John Gower, *Confessio Amantis*, Vol. 1, ed. Russell A. Peck (2000); Vol. 2 (2003)

Richard the Redeless and *Mum and the Sothsegger*, ed. James Dean (2000)

Ancrene Wisse, ed. Robert Hasenfratz (2000)

Walter Hilton, *The Scale of Perfection*, ed. Thomas Bestul (2000)

John Lydgate, *The Siege of Thebes*, ed. Robert Edwards (2001)

Pearl, ed. Sarah Stanbury (2001)

The Trials and Joys of Marriage, ed. Eve Salisbury (2002)

Middle English Legends of Women Saints, ed. Sherry L. Reames (2003)

The Wallace: Selections, ed. Anne McKim (2003)

Three Purgatory Poems (The Gast of Gy, Sir Owain, The Vision of Tundale), ed. Edward E. Foster (2004)

William Dunbar, *The Complete Works*, ed. John Conlee (2004)

Chaucerian Dream Visions and Complaints, ed. Dana M. Symons (2004)

Other TEAMS Publications

Documents of Practice Series:

> *Love and Marriage in Late Medieval London*, selected, translated, and introduced by Shannon McSheffrey (1995)
>
> *Sources for the History of Medicine in Late Medieval England*, selected, introduced, and translated by Carole Rawcliffe (1995)
>
> *A Slice of Life: Selected Documents of Medieval English Peasant Experience*, edited, translated, and with an introduction by Edwin Brezette DeWindt (1996)
>
> *Regular Life: Monastic, Canonical, and Mendicant Rules*, selected with an introduction by Douglas J. McMillan and Kathryn Smith Fladenmuller (1997); second edition, selected and introduced by Daniel Marcel La Corte and Douglas J. McMillan (2004)
>
> *Women and Monasticism in Medieval Europe: Sisters and Patrons of the Cistercian Reform*, selected, translated, and with an introduction by Constance H. Berman (2002)
>
> *Medieval Notaries and Their Acts: The 1327–1328 Register of Jean Holanie*, introduced, edited, and translated by Kathryn L. Reyerson and Debra A. Salata (2004)

Commentary Series:

> *Commentary on the Book of Jonah, Haimo of Auxerre*, translated with an introduction by Deborah Everhart (1993)

Medieval Exegesis in Translation: Commentaries on the Book of Ruth, translated with an introduction by Lesley Smith (1996)

Nicholas of Lyra's Apocalypse Commentary, translated with an introduction and notes by Philip D. W. Krey (1997)

Rabbi Ezra Ben Solomon of Gerona: Commentary on the Song of Songs and Other Kabbalistic Commentaries, selected, translated, and annotated by Seth Brody (1999)

John Wyclif: On the Truth of Holy Scripture, translated with an introduction and notes by Ian Christopher Levy (2001)

Second Thessalonians: Two Early Medieval Apocalyptic Commentaries, translated with an introduction by Steven R. Cartwright and Kevin L. Hughes (2001)

The Glossa Ordinaria *on the Song of Songs*, translated with an introduction and notes by Mary Dove (2004)

Medieval German Texts in Bilingual Editions Series:

Sovereignty and Salvation in the Vernacular, 1050–1150, introduction, translation, and notes by James A. Schultz (2000)

Ava's New Testament Narratives: "When the Old Law Passed Away," introduction, translations, and notes by James A. Rushing, Jr. (2003)

History as Literature: German World Chronicles of the Thirteenth Century in Verse, introduction, translations, and notes by R. Graeme Dunphy (2003)

To order please contact: MEDIEVAL INSTITUTE PUBLICATIONS
Western Michigan University
Kalamazoo, MI 49008–5432
Phone (269) 387–8755
FAX (269) 387–8750

http://www.wmich.edu/medieval/mip/index.html

Medieval Institute Publications is a program
of The Medieval Institute, College of Arts
and Sciences, Western Michigan University

Typeset in 10.5 pt. Times New Roman
with Times New Roman display
Manufactured by Cushing-Malloy, Inc.—Ann Arbor, Michigan

Medieval Institute Publications
College of Arts and Sciences
Western Michigan University
1903 W. Michigan Avenue
Kalamazoo, Michigan 49008-5432
www.wmich.edu/medieval/mip/

 WESTERN MICHIGAN UNIVERSITY